"The Supremes"

PETER LANG

New York • Washington, D.C./Baltimore • Bern
Frankfurt am Main • Berlin • Brussels • Vienna • Oxford

Barbara A. Perry

"The Supremes"

An Introduction to the U.S. Supreme Court Justices

SECOND EDITION

PETER LANG
New York • Washington, D.C./Baltimore • Bern
Frankfurt am Main • Berlin • Brussels • Vienna • Oxford

Library of Congress Cataloging-in-Publication Data

Perry, Barbara A. (Barbara Ann).
The supremes: an introduction to the U.S. Supreme Court Justices /
Barbara A. Perry.
p. cm.
Includes bibliographical references and index.
1. Judges—United States—Biography. 2. United States.
Supreme Court—Officials and employees—Biography. I. Title.
KF8744.P46   347.73'2634—dc22 [B]   2008036341
ISBN 978-0-8204-9548-4

Bibliographic information published by **Die Deutsche Bibliothek**.
Die Deutsche Bibliothek lists this publication in the "Deutsche
Nationalbibliografie"; detailed bibliographic data is available
on the Internet at http://dnb.ddb.de/.

Cover design by Nona Reuter

Informal group image of **Current Supreme Court Justices**
(March 2006), photographed by Steve Petteway, Supreme Court.

The paper in this book meets the guidelines for permanence and durability
of the Committee on Production Guidelines for Book Longevity
of the Council of Library Resources.

© 2009 Peter Lang Publishing, Inc., New York
29 Broadway, 18th floor, New York, NY 10006
www.peterlang.com

Printed in the United States of America

For my brothers, sisters-in-law, and niece
David, Ellen, and Jennifer Perry
and
Doug and Gayl Perry

Acknowledgments

In 1975, when I took my very first course in constitutional history with the late Mary Kay Tachau at the University of Louisville, she showed our class the famous 1968 CBS television interview that Justice Hugo Black had filmed with Eric Sevareid and Martin Agronsky. From that moment, constitutional law, and the black-robed Supreme Court jurists who interpret it, captivated me. At the Smithsonian the next year, I saw on display Justice Black's judicial robe and the famous dog-eared copy of the Constitution that he always carried in his breast pocket. I excitedly wrote a postcard to Dr. Tachau telling her of my discovery as if I had seen the sacred relics of a revered saint.

It seemed as though I had reached nirvana when I interviewed most of the Court's members in the mid-1980s for my dissertation research. That experience was surpassed only by my year-long stint as a judicial fellow at the Supreme Court in 1994–95, where I had the chance to observe the justices frequently in oral argument and personal conversations. My duties as a fellow at the Court included briefing visiting dignitaries and students; inevitably they would ask about the ideologies, personalities, and biographies of the nine members of the tribunal. When I returned to the classroom at Sweet Briar College, I had a fresh store of observations on the justices to share with my own students. For the past thirteen years, I have had the pleasure of teaching in the Supreme Court Summer Institute for Teachers, sponsored by the Supreme Court Historical Society and Street Law, which has given me the opportunity to meet with new justices and view them on the bench. It is a delight to share my knowledge with teachers from around the nation. I am thankful to all of these groups who requested more information on the jurists of America's highest court for planting the seed that a brief book would be welcome on the subject.

I am particularly grateful to Owen Lancer who, while at Peter Lang Publishing, suggested the format for this text. As the series editor, Professor David Schultz offered his wise counsel and expertise on the Court. Peter Lang's Phyllis Korper has been a faithful and patient editor, allowing me flexibility to write when it suited my very busy schedule that included a fellowship at the University of Louisville's McConnell Center in 2006–07.

Professor Henry Abraham's admirable model of scholarship, encyclopedic knowledge of the Court, and perennially optimistic support were crucial to my bringing this project to fruition. In the absence of my dear parents, my brothers and their families have been a dependable source of concern, understanding, and happiness. This book is dedicated to them with gratitude and love.

Contents

Introduction

The title of this book of essays on contemporary members of the Supreme Court of the United States will perhaps recall the popular Motown singing trio led by Diana Ross in the 1960s, but the title is meant to convey the obvious supremacy of the highest court in the land and the demonstrable merit of the tribunal's members in the early twenty-first century.

Most observers agree that the justices who currently occupy the black leather chairs behind the Supreme Court's mahogany bench are among the most capable to serve the tribunal since the Roosevelt Court in the 1940s. As of 2008, the Court's membership included, in order of seniority, with the chief justice first:

- John G. Roberts, Jr. (nominated by George W. Bush in 2005);
- John Paul Stevens (nominated by Gerald Ford in 1975);
- Antonin Scalia (nominated by Ronald Reagan in 1986);
- Anthony M. Kennedy (appointed by Ronald Reagan in 1988);
- David H. Souter (nominated by George H. W. Bush in 1990);
- Clarence Thomas (nominated by George H. W. Bush in 1991);
- Ruth Bader Ginsburg (nominated by Bill Clinton in 1993);
- Stephen G. Breyer (nominated by Bill Clinton in 1994);
- Samuel A. Alito, Jr. (appointed by George W. Bush in 2006).

Their educational backgrounds are superb. Roberts and Souter received both their undergraduate and law degrees from Harvard. Kennedy and Breyer attended Stanford as undergraduates and then moved on to Harvard Law School, where Scalia also received his law degree. Ruth Bader Ginsburg earned her bachelor's degree from Cornell, studied law for two years at Harvard, and completed her law degree at Columbia after she moved to New York to be with her husband. Thomas and Scalia attended Catholic institutions for undergraduate studies— Holy Cross and Georgetown, respectively; Thomas went on to Yale Law School as did Alito, who was an undergraduate at Princeton. Stevens, with deep roots in the Windy City, attended the University of Chicago and Northwestern Law School.

Two justices did postgraduate work at Oxford (Souter on a Rhodes Scholarship, Breyer on a Marshall Scholarship). Kennedy studied at the London School of Economics. Most would have been considered classic "overachievers," having received stellar grades and graduating at or near the top of their classes. Six were elected to Phi Beta Kappa as undergraduates (Roberts, Stevens, Kennedy, Souter, Ginsburg, and Breyer); two-thirds served on law reviews (Roberts, Stevens, Scalia, Ginsburg, Breyer, and Alito).

The nine justices also brought a range of political, governmental, and judicial experience to the Supreme Court. The Reagan administration placed a premium on previous court service, especially at the federal level, and succeeding presidents have also used that selection criterion. No member of the present Court has ascended the bench without previous experience as a federal judge. Roberts, Stevens, and Breyer had been Supreme Court clerks, for William Rehnquist, Wiley Rutledge, and Arthur Goldberg, respectively. Souter possessed extensive state court experience in New Hampshire. Kennedy, Ginsburg, Breyer, and Alito all had tenures of a dozen years or more on the U.S. circuit courts. Stevens and Scalia each spent five years on the federal appeals tribunals; Roberts had two years there. Souter and Thomas briefly served on the U.S. circuit benches just prior to their appointments to the Supreme Court. Experience in all three branches of the federal government before coming to the high court gives Justices Thomas and Breyer the edge in breadth of previous public service. Chief Justice Roberts and Justice Kennedy possess the most experience in private law practice (thirteen and fourteen years, respectively). Roberts and Alito had extensive service in the executive branch. Roberts was a special assistant to the attorney general and principal deputy solicitor general in the Department of Justice. The future chief justice also served as an associate counsel to President Reagan in the White House Counsel's Office. Alito was assistant to the U.S. solicitor general and deputy assistant to the attorney general. He also had the most prosecutorial experience before arriving at the Supreme Court, as assistant U.S. attorney and U.S. attorney, both in New Jersey. Justice Thomas held two appointed positions in the federal government (at the Department of Education and the Equal Employment Opportunity Commission) before his first judgeship. Academe was Justice Ginsburg's proving ground for the federal bench, and Justices Kennedy and Breyer have taught extensively as adjunct professors. Scalia's résumé reflects a background of teaching law, executive branch service, think tank research, and private practice.

In its social characteristics, the Supreme Court of the early twenty-first century can hardly be said to "look like America," but it is far more "representative" than in the distant past. Today's Court has only one female member. The "black seat," established in 1967 with Thurgood Marshall's appointment, remained intact (albeit controversial) with Clarence Thomas's 1991 nomination. Only recently did the Court achieve a majority of members from minority religious groups: Roberts, Kennedy, Scalia, Thomas, and Alito are Roman Catholic; Ginsburg and Breyer are Jewish. To have a majority of Catholics on the high bench is unprecedented. Souter is Episcopalian, and Stevens does not belong to any particular Christian denomination. In geographic terms, this bench is fairly balanced. Kennedy and Breyer hail from northern California. Scalia and Ginsburg were raised in New York, Alito in New Jersey, and Souter in New England. Roberts and Stevens are Midwesterners. Clarence Thomas is the only Southerner on this Court. Of course, in some cases, careers and lifestyle choices have taken the justices far from their roots. Stevens spends considerable time at his Florida home, and Breyer still maintains a home near Boston, where he served on the U.S. First Circuit Court of Appeals. Roberts has spent virtually all of his adult life on the East Coast and now has a summer home in Maine. Ginsburg lived for thirteen years in Washington as a judge on the U.S. Court of Appeals for the District of Columbia. As of 2008, the average age of the justices was 68.5: Stevens was the oldest at 88, Ginsburg 75, Kennedy and Scalia 72, Breyer 70, Souter 69, Thomas 60, Alito 58, and Roberts 53.

While most of the current justices came from middle- or upper-middle-class households and enjoyed numerous advantages in making their way up the educational and professional ladder, two had to overcame societal discrimination to achieve their positions on the nation's highest court. Ginsburg faced gender-based handicaps at the outset of her career. Although she graduated at the top of her Ivy League law school class, she was not offered a prized Supreme Court clerkship, nor could she find an associate's position in New York law firms. Ginsburg procured a clerkship with a U.S. district court judge through her mentor, Professor Gerald Gunther, and then became a law professor. Justice Thomas overcame a poverty-stricken early childhood to advance through Yale Law School's affirmative action program, only to be denied a position in law firms; he began his career in the Missouri attorney general's office. Several members of the current Court have triumphed over personal tragedies and hardships. As a teenager, Ruth Bader Ginsburg lost her mother to cancer and then nursed her husband through testicular cancer while they both were in law school. She successfully battled her colorectal cancer a decade ago. Early in his career, Justice Kennedy's father died prematurely of a heart attack, and then Kennedy's mother, sister, and brother passed away in quick succession. In 2006 Kennedy had a second stent inserted in a blood vessel near his heart to prop open an artery that doctors had unclogged. Justice Thomas's father abandoned his family when Thomas was a young boy, and he and his brother were raised by their strict grandparents. Thomas and Stevens have endured divorces; both remarried. Chief Justice Roberts seemed to lead a charmed life until a frightening seizure hospitalized him in 2007. The public learned that it was his second such episode in fourteen years, but doctors reportedly could not pinpoint any diagnosable reason for them. A pack of young thugs set upon Justice Souter while he jogged through Washington streets in 2004, but his injuries were minor. Court police officers could find no evidence that the street hooligans even recognized their famous victim, a testament to why most justices prefer not to allow cameras to televise their public sessions!

In oral arguments, the current justices constitute one of the liveliest benches in recent memory. All but Thomas are frequent, persistent, and incisive questioners. Moreover, this Supreme Court contains some of the wittiest inquisitors the hallowed courtroom has ever witnessed. Increasingly, the sober, church-like atmosphere there is interrupted by laughter when Roberts makes a wry observation, Scalia delivers a sarcastic one-liner, Souter utters a droll quip in his New England accent, or Breyer presents an ironic, professorial comment. With their rapier-like intellects and wits, these justices have made oral argument sessions unexpectedly entertaining, as well as edifying, events.

Jurisprudential and ideological labels are imprecise at best, but most observers agree on general categories and descriptions of the current justices' voting postures. From right to left on the political spectrum, Justices Scalia and Thomas are considered the most conservative, with their commitment to a text-based, original understanding of the Constitution. Chief Justice Roberts and Justice Alito, both life-long conservatives, represent the cultural conservatism of George W. Bush. They eschewed overarching judicial theories in their Senate confirmation hearings but claimed respect for precedent and narrow interpretations of statutes and the Constitution. Roberts has publicly expressed a desire to decrease the number of 5–4 rulings. "Why don't you come along with a very narrow opinion. We can get seven votes for that. It will look a lot better," Scalia has quoted the new chief imploring his colleagues. In the category of moderate-conservative "swing voter," Justice Kennedy prides himself on his considered, sometimes agonizing, case-by-case approach to decisions. The most common voting alignment in narrowly decided rulings has recently consisted of Chief Justice Roberts and Justices Kennedy, Scalia, Thomas, and Alito.

No social liberals in the William Brennan or Thurgood Marshall image remain on the Court, but Justice Souter has often followed in the footsteps of his late friend Justice Brennan. Justices Souter, Stevens, Ginsburg, and Breyer frequently side as a liberal bloc, and, if they can attract a fifth vote (usually Kennedy), will win, as they have in terrorist detainee rights, juvenile death penalty, and environmental cases. Justices Ginsburg and Breyer are deemed moderate liberals for their reluctance to impose highly activist standards even when they reach a liberal decision. Justice Stevens's sometimes maverick approach to the law can oblige him to write solo dissents or concurrences. His seniority, however, means that when the chief justice is in dissent and Stevens is in the majority, he can write the opinion for the Court himself or assign it to a colleague.

The Roberts-led Court, with his fellow Bush II appointee Justice Alito, has only been in place for a full term since 2006–07. Along with the preceding Rehnquist Court, it has modified and occasionally rolled back precedents of the Warren and Burger eras. Abortion remains legal, with some limits on access to the procedure, including a national ban on partial-birth methods; organized, state-sponsored prayer in public schools remains unlawful, but states can display the Ten Commandments under certain conditions; free-exercise-of-religion claims have been upheld but not if general secular laws impinge on those claims only incidentally; free speech and press continue to lie at the heart of American democracy, except for students, child pornographers, and some campaign finance laws; affirmative action programs are constitutional if they meet the highest level of judicial scrutiny, which race-based public school assignments do not; majority-minority voting districts are also subject to strict scrutiny; gender classifications trigger a lower standard of scrutiny but generally have been nullified; statutory procedures for determining gender-based pay inequity have been narrowly interpreted; homosexual activity is now protected under privacy rights; criminal rights have been somewhat diluted, especially in the search-and-seizure category, and public school students in extracurricular activities may be subjected to random drug-testing; capital punishment is unconstitutional for mentally retarded or juvenile defendants and child rapists; lethal-injection protocols have been upheld; statutes passed under Congress's interstate commerce power have fared poorly; and presidential power regarding alleged terrorists has been limited.

Although its docket has shrunk by more than half since the 1980s for a variety of reasons,[1] the Supreme Court remains the jewel in the crown of the American governmental system. Indeed, it is the envy of judiciaries worldwide for its leadership of an independent judicial branch, for the professionalism and integrity of its members, and for the dignity of its public procedures and symbolism. Not surprisingly, it consistently scores higher than Congress or the presidency in polls measuring public confidence in governmental institutions. It did so even after its divisive *Bush v. Gore* decision that settled the 2000 presidential election. As Justice David Souter describes the Supreme Court's exalted status in the American polity: "Most people are willing to accept the fact that the Court tries to play it straight. That acceptance has been built up by the preceding hundred justices . . . going back to the beginning. We are, in fact, trading on the good faith and the conscientiousness of the justices who went before us. The power of the Court is the power of trust earned—the trust of the American people."[2]

CHAPTER ONE

John G. Roberts, Jr.

At the end of June 2006, Washington, D.C., endured several days of thunderstorms and torrential rains as a tropical depression stalled over the mid-Atlantic coast. The nation's capital was inundated. Even the venerable National Archives, home to the U.S. Constitution, had to close, falling victim to a flooded basement that knocked out its utilities. Characteristically, the Supreme Court forged ahead. It remained open while the justices and their clerks put the finishing touches on the final opinions for the 2005–06 term. As its session drew to a close for the summer, Chief Justice John Roberts, who was completing his first term at the Court's helm, met one evening with a group of social studies teachers from around the nation. Looking a bit bedraggled after sloshing to the Court building, they gathered in one of the high tribunal's ornate ceremonial conference rooms to hear the new chief justice speak to them at the culmination of their week-long seminar on the Supreme Court.

Roberts entered the room with two plain-clothes members of the Court's police force and headed for the podium. A little less than six feet tall, he does not cut quite the imposing figure that his predecessor, the lanky William Rehnquist, did. In fact, he has an all-American look and an approachable persona. If Hollywood were to produce a movie about his life, Tom Hanks could well approximate the young-looking chief justice's characteristics. Roberts immediately put the teachers at ease with an endearing declaration, "Welcome to *your* Court." Their comfort level increased as he recounted an anecdote to which all parents in the group could relate. "The chief," as employees of the Court traditionally refer to their leader, stated that the previous evening he set out to buy provisions for his two young children to take to camp. Thinking he would avoid the deluge by parking in an underground garage, he came out of the store only to find that the water was ankle-deep between him and his car. Not wanting to ruin his shoes, he took the plastic shopping bags, tied them around his feet, rolled up his trousers to the knee, and began wading to his auto. The teachers, already chuckling at this absurd picture in their mind's eye, burst into laughter when Roberts delivered his punch line, "I was glad there were no photographers around to record that image of the chief justice!"[1]

Yet Roberts's "Everyman" demeanor and warm charm do not veil his intellectual genius, incisive understanding of the law, or firm leadership displayed on the nation's highest court. Though born in Buffalo, New York, on January 27, 1955, to John Glover Roberts, Sr., and Rosemary Padrasky, young John and his three sisters grew up in Long Beach, Indiana, a prosperous town on the shores of Lake Michigan. As a steel company executive, John Sr. provided a comfortable lifestyle for his Roman Catholic family. John attended parochial schools for his primary and secondary education. At Notre Dame Catholic School, his eighth-grade math teacher recognized his brilliance but noted that the youngster was not boastful about his intellect. John applied to La Lumiere, a demanding Catholic prep school for boys in nearby La Porte, Indiana. He described his ambition to finish ahead of his peers in a competitive scholastic atmosphere so that he could pursue "the best job." John followed through on his goal, excelling in the classroom and on the playing field, where he served as co-captain of the football team. In addition, his extracurricular activities included co-editing the student newspaper, singing in the choir, acting in drama productions, and serving on the student council.

Despite his busy life outside the classroom, Roberts received the highest grades in each of his years at La Lumiere. In his calculus class, when everyone else earned Ds or Fs on a test, John garnered a perfect score. He thrived on the strict discipline imposed at the institution, where he assisted the priests in preparing for Mass. Graduating first among the school's twenty-five seniors, Roberts gained a spot in the 1973 entering freshman class at Harvard, where he completed his undergraduate history major in only three years. Even more impressive was his earning a bachelor's degree *summa cum laude*, as well as Phi Beta Kappa honors, in the highly competitive Ivy League university. His senior thesis, on British liberalism in the twentieth century, received a prize for best in the graduating class. Despite his burnished résumé, Roberts maintained his modest, mid-western temperament, perhaps humbled by his summer jobs in the Indiana steel mills. He also held firmly to the conservative values instilled by his family, church, and parochial schools.

Roberts continued to build on his solid educational foundation by enrolling in Harvard Law School the fall after his graduation from college. He again distinguished himself by serving as the managing editor of the *Harvard Law Review* and graduating *magna cum laude* in 1979—all the while holding on to his conservative outlook and lifestyle, despite Harvard's liberal reputation as "Moscow on the Charles [River]." His roommate recalled years later that Roberts was never aggressive about his ideology, but "I just knew he was conservative across the board. It just came across whenever we would get to talking about movies or politics. . . ."[2] The editor of the law review observed that Roberts never even experimented with his choice of ice cream flavors, predictably choosing chocolate chip every time!

His stellar dossier resulted in a clerkship with one of the nation's most esteemed federal judges, Henry J. Friendly, of the U.S. Court of Appeals for the Second Circuit in New York City. An Eisenhower appointee, Friendly was a conservative Republican who advocated judicial restraint and deference to the political branches of government. Roberts then moved to the plum clerkship coveted by all new lawyers with prestigious credentials and dreams of careers on top of the law hierarchy—at the U.S. Supreme Court. His mentor there was then-Associate Justice William H. Rehnquist. They forged a strong professional link and warm friendship, whose bond would last until Rehnquist's death in 2005. By then, Rehnquist had served as the chief justice for nearly two decades, and Roberts was one of the pallbearers who carried his mentor's casket up the Court's majestic marble steps to lie in repose in the building's Great Hall.

By the time Roberts completed his Supreme Court clerkship in 1981, President Ronald Reagan had just begun his eight-year presidency, a fortuitous turn of events for young conservatives. The ascendency of America's political right opened multiple career paths to youthful politicos and lawyers who flocked to Washington. Roberts's first position was as assistant to Reagan's attorney general William French Smith from 1981 to 1982. During his short tenure at the Department of Justice, Roberts witnessed Reagan's historic nomination of the first woman to the U.S. Supreme Court, Sandra Day O'Connor. Roberts prepared a memo for the nominee assuring her that "the proposition that the only way Senators can ascertain a nominee's views is through questions on specific cases should be rejected."[3] He also defended the Reagan administration's anti-busing stance, asserting that busing failed to achieve its goal of desegregation when parents transferred their children to private schools to avoid the policy.

Following his short stint with the attorney general, Roberts moved several blocks up Pennsylvania Avenue to serve as the associate counsel to the president, where he stayed for four years under President Reagan's chief counsel, Fred Fielding. While in the White House Counsel's Office, Roberts wrote a memo to Fielding supporting a Senate bill to ban busing, which he repeated was counter-productive to achieving integration because of "white flight" from public schools. In other memos, he justified the Reagan administration's opposition to affirmative action for women and provided support for contending that the federal courts should not apply a heightened standard of scrutiny to government-imposed gender classifications.

In 1986 Roberts left government service for three years to practice in the oldest and largest Washington law firm of Hogan & Hartson, where he achieved partner in appellate litigation after only a year. As a court-appointed counsel for a defendant asserting his right against double jeopardy, he won the very first case he argued at the U.S. Supreme Court, *United States v. Halper*, in 1989 by a unanimous vote. He then moved back to the Department of Justice, where he served as the principal deputy solicitor general until 1993 under the presidency of George H. W. Bush.

With conservative Kenneth Starr leading the solicitor general's office, Roberts became a trusted advocate for the Bush administration's position before the Supreme Court in both oral arguments with the justices and written legal briefs submitted to them. He co-authored a brief in *Rust v. Sullivan*, the 1991 case involving the so-called "gag rule" that prohibited federally funded family planning clinics from discussing the option of abortion with clients. He argued for the U.S. government that it could ban funding to any clinic that provided abortions or counseled clients about the procedure. Such bans did not violate the First Amendment rights of such clinics because the government may selectively fund programs as it sees fit, Roberts's brief contended. A majority of the justices agreed with Roberts's argument. They did not, however, act on a footnote in his brief maintaining that "*Roe* [*v. Wade*] was wrongly decided and should be overruled" because the Constitution did not support a woman's fundamental right to an abortion.[4] On other First Amendment issues, Deputy Solicitor General Roberts argued that clergy-led prayers at public school graduations did not violate the Establishment Clause and that a federal law banning flag burning did not contravene free speech rights. The Supreme Court disagreed with both positions, as they would with another Roberts-authored brief for the government opposing affirmative action in the Federal Communications Commission's preference for minority-owned stations in granting licenses. Although the high court did not always accept his positions for the government, he made the most of his four years in the s.g.'s office by honing his advocacy skills before the tribunal, whose justices respected his sharp intellect paired with a genial personality.

These skills did not go unnoticed by the Bush judicial appointments team, and the president nominated thirty-seven-year-old Roberts to the U.S. Court of Appeals for the D.C. Circuit in 1992, just before the president's reelection defeat. Nominations to the federal bench often languish at the end of a lame-duck presidency, especially if the Senate is in the hands of the opposition party. Fearing that the talented Mr. Roberts was being groomed by Republicans for a future Supreme Court vacancy, Democrats were only too happy to scuttle his appointment to the D.C. Circuit, which is traditionally a stepping-stone to the nation's highest court. His nomination never received an up-or-down Senate vote.

When President Bill Clinton moved into the White House in 1993, Roberts returned to private practice at Hogan & Hartson, where he settled in for the duration of the Democrat's two-term presidency. Resuming his partnership at the prestigious corporate law firm, he led its appellate division and argued frequently before the Supreme Court. In 1996 he married Jane Sullivan, a corporate attorney at another Washington law firm. Also a conservative Catholic, who was a member of the anti-abortion Feminists for Life, Jane met her future husband through mutual friends. Four years later they adopted two children, Josie and Jack, within a few months of each other.

Although Roberts's client base at Hogan was primarily corporate, he provided his appellate expertise in the mid-1990s free of charge to gay rights advocates before the Supreme Court. Roberts did not argue the case or write briefs, but he offered strategic advice and imparted legal theories as well as coached the advocates in moot court sessions. The case, *Romer v. Evans*, decided by the justices in 1996, set a precedent for banning state-imposed restrictions on anti-discrimination laws for gays. While Roberts's *pro bono* contributions to this landmark litigation for gay rights seemed at odds with his conservative background, a close friend of Roberts at the law firm, the eminent Supreme Court advocate, E. Barrett Prettyman, Jr., recalled that, although he had scores of lunches with his colleague over the years, he could not recall a single time in which Roberts had tipped his hand regarding politics.

Yet during the tumultuous recount of Florida votes in the aftermath of the contentious 2000 presidential election between Vice President Al Gore and Texas Governor George W. Bush, Roberts worked behind the scenes advising Bush's lawyers. He also counseled Florida Governor Jeb Bush (George's brother) on how the state legislature could help swing Florida's crucial electoral votes to the Republican candidate should courts decide otherwise. Ultimately, litigation over the controversy reached the U.S. Supreme Court, which stopped the Sunshine

State's recount and effectively gave Bush the victory. A year later the new president repeated his father's gesture and nominated Roberts to the U.S. Court of Appeals for the D.C. Circuit. Again, Senate Democrats blocked his appointment in the Judiciary Committee. In 2002, however, Republicans regained the committee's majority and shepherded Roberts's nomination to the full Senate. Without opposition, a voice vote confirmed his appointment to the D.C. Circuit on May 8, 2003. By virtue of his stellar record and golden reputation, he now became a natural addition to the Bush administration's short list should a vacancy occur on the high court.

Over the next two years, Judge Roberts would write nearly fifty opinions. His rulings rarely drew dissents from his colleagues on the D.C. Circuit; likewise, he infrequently issued dissenting opinions. Some observers have noted that these statistics indicate that he takes a narrow view of the law, avoiding the sweeping judgments of more liberal judges, which might attract more dissents. His conservative tendencies appeared in his first opinion, a dissent from the circuit's decision not to reconsider a three-judge panel's ruling protecting a toad under the Endangered Species Act. Roberts wanted to give a developer in California, whose business had been trumped by the "hapless toad" a chance to argue before the entire circuit that the panel had erred in its application of the pro-environment legislation.

One of Roberts's rulings drew national attention in a case that arose from a seemingly trivial incident involving a twelve-year-old girl eating a french fry in a Washington, D.C., subway station. In applying a "zero tolerance" policy against riders eating and drinking in the city's underground transportation system that prides itself on cleanliness, the Metro Transit police arrested the french-fry-nibbling scofflaw. They searched and handcuffed the frightened child, removed her shoelaces, and transported her in the windowless compartment of a police vehicle to a juvenile processing center where she was held for three hours until her mother arrived. Eventually, she initiated a federal civil rights suit on her daughter's behalf, claiming a violation of her Fourth and Fifth Amendment rights. The mother asserted, in particular, that her child's equal protection guarantees had been violated because the Metro policy allowed for citations to be issued to *adult* violators but required *juveniles* to be arrested. In fact, the negative reaction to the police force's heavy-handed tactics directed at the pre-teen forced a revision of the policy to require citation only for both adults and children who dared eat or drink in the Washington subway system.

When the case reached the D.C. circuit, Judge Roberts, writing for a unanimous three-judge panel, upheld the U.S. district court's ruling against the mother. While noting that the whole incident was unfortunate, he determined that the appropriateness of the policy was not the question before the court. Rather, he ruled that the no-citation policy resulting in the child's arrest was rationally related to the Metro's goal of involving parents in the delinquent actions of their children. Roberts noted that juveniles might provide fictitious names to officers who could only issue them a citation.

In another circuit court case involving government power over individuals, Judge Roberts wrote for a 2–1 majority that the federal Commodity Futures and Trading Commission did not owe attorneys' fees to plaintiffs who had won their case against the commission. Overturning a magistrate judge's decision to award the fees under the Equal Access to Justice Act, Roberts concluded that the commission's position in the litigation was adequately justified (despite its losing the case) to bar the award.

Judge Roberts was on the losing side of a circuit court case in which he once more voted in favor of governmental power, this time to the benefit of police in the criminal justice realm. He dissented from the two-judge majority that overturned the conviction of a defendant for carrying an illegal gun and ammunition in the trunk of a car. The majority argued that the car search by U.S. Park Police violated the driver's Fourth Amendment rights against unreasonable search and seizure. The police had stopped the driver for having an inoperable license plate light, whereupon they discovered the car contained stolen temporary tags and was not registered in Virginia, from which the driver's license had been suspended. He told the police that the car belonged to his girlfriend, who had only recently purchased the vehicle at an auction. The officers did not share with him their suspicion that the car was stolen; rather, they simply proceeded to search the trunk and discovered the gun and ammunition. The majority contended that the police should have sought more information from the driver and given him the opportunity to prove his story by having his girlfriend come to the scene with proof of ownership. Roberts's dissent challenged the practicality of such a conclusion and, with characteristic wit, he maintained, "Sometimes a car being driven by an unlicensed driver, with no registration and stolen tags, really does belong to the driver's friend, and sometimes dogs do eat homework, but in neither case is it reasonable to insist on checking out the story before taking other appropriate action."[5]

Although the George W. Bush administration had considered Judge Roberts an obvious choice for the nation's highest court, a vacancy was very slow in coming. The president's first term passed without a retirement among the jurists, though their average age was seventy. The justices sitting on the bench when the U.S. Supreme Court ended its 2004–05 term in June 2005 had been together eleven years, the longest serving group of nine ever (since the Court's size increased to that number in 1869). Only a smaller Court in the 1820s had served longer without a vacancy. Yet it was clear from the Court's last session on that hot June morning in 2005 that a seat would soon come open, and it probably would be the center chair. Chief Justice Rehnquist was battling the latter stages of thyroid cancer, and he could barely speak as he announced the Court's opinion upholding the display of the Ten Commandments on Texas's state capitol grounds. With a tube implanted in his throat, he was barely able to utter a few whispered words stating the Court's ruling and a brief rationale. Veteran journalists who had covered the Court for years blinked away tears as they witnessed what they assumed would be the chief's last appearance on the high bench after more than three decades at the Marble Temple.

A few weeks previously, his colleague, Justice O'Connor had approached the chief justice, her long-time friend and former date (when they both were attending Stanford Law School in the 1950s). Although seventy-five years of age, the first woman justice's health was excellent, despite treatment for breast cancer in 1988. Yet John O'Connor, her husband of more than fifty years, was slipping deeper into Alzheimer's. In its earlier stages, she would bring him to the Court each day and watch over him in her chambers, but the disease's steady progress was making that arrangement unfeasible. Despite her boundless energy and devotion to the high court she had served with such dedication since 1981, she told Rehnquist that she was considering retiring, perhaps after one more term on the bench. As a cancer survivor, she was certainly sensitive to the chief's health problems and had witnessed firsthand his determination to carry on even as the disease and chemotherapy ravaged his body. Nevertheless, she thought he might indicate to her that he was contemplating retirement after the 2004–05 term ended. To her surprise, he did not. In fact, he communicated his intention to stay another year and emphasized that the Court could ill afford two retirements at the same time. Therefore, she was left with no other choice but to leave a year earlier than she had initially anticipated.

As the nation's capital awaited what it thought would be Rehnquist's retirement announcement after the term ended in June 2005, none came. Washington's denizens were heading out of town in anticipation of a long, quiet 4th of July weekend when Justice O'Connor's Friday morning announcement on July 1, 2005, stunned them and the country. She wrote to President Bush that she intended to retire from the bench "upon the nomination and confirmation of my successor. It has been a great privilege, indeed, to have served as a member of the Court for 24 Terms. I will leave it with enormous respect for the integrity of the Court and its role under our Constitutional structure." After receiving her letter, hand-carried to the White House by the Court's marshal, Bush phoned O'Connor to declare to the Arizonan who grew up on a ranch, "For an old ranching girl, you turned out pretty good." Known for his paradoxical behavior as a tough-talking Texan, who can turn tearfully sentimental, Bush gushed, "I wish I was there to hug you."[6]

Other conservatives were less maudlin; their overwhelming emotion upon hearing of O'Connor's departure was pure elation. Finally, they could glimpse the promised land where O'Connor's moderate swing vote would be replaced by a reliably conservative one. The media reported that the two frontrunners fitting this profile were John Roberts and Judge J. Michael Luttig of the 4th Circuit U.S. Court of Appeals. Judges J. Harvie Wilkinson III (4th Circuit) and Samuel Alito (3rd Circuit) were also considered contenders. Bush, however, wanted to consider his longtime Texas friend and advisor, Attorney General Alberto Gonzales, whom he had previously appointed to the Texas Supreme Court while the Lone Star State's governor. A graduate of Harvard Law School, former White House counsel, and a member of the president's Cabinet, Gonzales, the son of poor Mexican immigrants, certainly portrayed a compelling life story. If Bush chose him, he would be the first Hispanic to serve on the Supreme Court, a landmark that the president was anxious to establish. Yet conservatives exclaimed that "'Gonzales' was Spanish for [Justice David] 'Souter,'" a reference to President George H. W. Bush's 1990 nomination of the New Hampshire judge, presumed to be conservative, who then joined the Supreme Court's liberal bloc. The right side of the political spectrum did not trust Gonzales on affirmative action and abortion, two issues where O'Connor's replacement could help overturn liberal precedents forged by previous Courts. If Bush was determined to create a Hispanic seat, conservatives preferred Judge Emilio Garza of the 5th Circuit, considered more dependable by the right.

Other groups were more interested in replacing O'Connor with another woman, so that Justice Ruth Bader Ginsburg would not become the sole female on the nation's highest court. Some conservatives, as well as liberals, deemed the "woman's seat," established by Reagan with O'Connor's 1981 appointment, too historic to ignore. Conservative federal appeals court Judges Janice Rogers Brown (9th Circuit), Edith Jones (5th Circuit), and Edith Clement (11th Circuit) were mentioned as possible nominees should Bush decide that gender would be paramount in his criteria. First Lady Laura Bush urged him in that direction.

The president, attending a summit conference in Scotland, spoke publicly for the first time since O'Connor's announcement the previous week about his process for choosing his first Supreme Court nominee. "I will let my legal experts deal with the ramifications of legal opinions," he explained. "I will try to assess their character, their interests. I'll pick people who, one, can do the job, people who are honest, people who are bright, and people who will strictly interpret the Constitution and not use the bench to legislate from."[7]

Ultimately, the short list for O'Connor's seat included the quintet of Roberts, Luttig, Wilkinson, Alito, and Clement, all of whom the president personally interviewed at the White House. As most presidents do, Bush placed ideology at the top of his selection criteria list. Each of the finalists was conservative. Obviously, he had put ethnicity aside, and gender was not going to be the overriding factor in choosing O'Connor's successor. The president and his staff knew that they would sooner rather than later have another seat to fill when Rehnquist inevitably left the Court, either by his own decision or the Almighty's.

Roberts's arrival for his interview at the Executive Mansion exhibited a cloak and dagger element. He had hurried home from a teaching engagement in London to be hustled into the East Wing (rather than the West Wing where the press camps out) in order to preserve the secrecy surrounding the selection process. With all of the candidates, Bush initially engaged in pleasant banter in an attempt to diffuse the tension. "I know you don't do this every day," he commented to Roberts.[8] The chief executive, joined by his White House counsel, another friend from Texas, Harriet Miers, then segued into a dialogue on Roberts's view of judicial power and approaches to the law. A senior administration official told the *Washington Post* a few days later that the president and Judge Roberts "really clicked well. [Bush] relies on his intuition about people as well as his views on substantive issues. In this case, the stars aligned." Or, as another White House staffer described Roberts's performance, "He aced the interview."[9] Thus, the last piece of the selection puzzle dropped seamlessly into place. Roberts had it all: the stellar education at Harvard (times two), judicial clerkships with two of the most well-respected judges in the federal courts, government service in the executive branch, appellate advocacy at a prestigious Washington law firm, two years experience on the D.C. circuit, appropriate age (neither too untested, nor too old), a congenial and modest personality, and an ability to follow his conservative principles effectively, without aggression or belligerence. In a perfect coincidence, on the day of the interview, the D.C. Circuit announced its decision favoring the Bush administration's policy of trying terror suspects before military tribunals. Judge Roberts had signed on to the decision.

Still, Roberts had no inkling about what the result of his interview would be. He returned to London to complete his course. Yet he had barely been back in England a day when the White House phoned in the middle of the night to ask him to return to Washington, again without attracting attention. Making his third trans-Atlantic flight in fewer than ten days, Roberts landed bleary-eyed in the steamy Washington heat on July 19, 2005, and raced home just in time to receive the call from the president who revealed that he would nominate him that night at the White House.

After dinner at the mansion with President and Mrs. Bush, Roberts, surrounded by his wife Jane, daughter Josie, 5, and son Jack, 4, who danced in front of the East Room podium, looked on as his commander-in-chief named him the 109th justice of the U.S. Supreme Court. "In public service and in private practice," Bush reported, "he has argued thirty-nine cases before the Supreme Court and earned a reputation as one of the best legal minds of his generation. Judge Roberts has earned the respect of people from both political parties. . . . He's a man of extraordinary accomplishment and ability. He has a good heart. He has the qualities Americans expect in a judge: experience, wisdom, fairness, and civility."[10]

John Roberts stepped to the microphone to make a short statement of gratitude to the 43rd president of the United States for naming him to the high court. He spoke of arguing cases before the justices as an appellate advocate, which had given him "a profound appreciation for the role of the Court in our constitutional democracy and a deep regard for the institution." "I always got a lump in my throat whenever I walked up those marble steps [to the Court]," Roberts recalled, "and I don't think it was just from nerves." Gazing at his two young children, dressed in their Sunday best, he explained that they reminded him "every day why it's so important for us to work to preserve the institutions of our democracy."[11]

One of the first responses to Bush's choice came from the justice he was to replace. The media tracked down Justice O'Connor to a stream in Idaho, where she was fly-fishing. Wading in the water, wearing her fishing vest decorated with red feathered lures, the first woman justice called over her shoulder when asked about Roberts, "He's good in every way, except he's not a woman."[12] The public was more positive, with nearly two-thirds polled responding that the Senate should confirm him. But a slightly higher majority said that he should express his views on abortion.

Responses on Capitol Hill to Roberts's nomination were predictably partisan: Democratic Senate Minority Leader Harry M. Reid (D.-Nev.) acknowledged the federal judge's "suitable legal credentials" but noted that the Senate had to "determine if he has a demonstrated commitment to the core American values of freedom, equality, and fairness." Reid's counterpart, Republican Majority Leader Bill Frist (R.-Tenn.) proclaimed Roberts "the kind of outstanding nominee that will make America proud."[13] As Roberts began making courtesy calls on senators, the Senate Judiciary Committee scheduled hearings on his nomination for just after the Labor Day weekend. The Bush administration reasoned that, if the Senate confirmed Roberts in a timely fashion, he could assume O'Connor's seat by the start of the Court's 2005–06 term the first Monday in October. In the meantime, senators, their staffs, interest groups, and the general public contemplated the ramifications of Roberts's long paper trail, as an executive branch official in the Reagan and Bush I administrations, an appellate lawyer in private practice, and a federal jurist. The White House tried to withhold some of Roberts's papers from his service in the Bush I administration, arguing that they were privileged internal executive branch documents. This Supreme Court nomination, the first in over a decade, was also the first since the widespread use of the Internet; many of Roberts's memos, briefs, and opinions were now available online for anyone to read.

Just as Washington was starting a federal holiday weekend when Justice O'Connor announced her retirement, the nation's capital was in the first day of the Labor Day holiday, anticipating the start of Roberts's confirmation hearings before the Senate Judiciary Committee on Tuesday, when word arrived that Chief Justice Rehnquist had succumbed to his cancer late on Saturday evening. His demise upended the judicial politics playboard. Would Bush promote sitting Justices Antonin Scalia or Clarence Thomas, two judges he had often admiringly cited, to the chief justiceship? Or would he go back to his short list for the O'Connor vacancy or search beyond it for the next chief justice? The media began to speculate about Alito, Clement, Garza, Gonzales, Jones, Luttig, and Wilkinson, while some senators debated whether to postpone the Roberts hearings for a week out of respect for Rehnquist and in light of the Hurricane Katrina disaster along the Gulf coast.

Before that decision on Capitol Hill could be made, President Bush quickly nominated Roberts to serve as the seventeenth chief justice of the United States. This time in the Oval Office, with only Roberts by his side, Bush explained in his televised statement that he wanted to ensure that a new chief justice was in the Court's center chair when it began its new term on October 3. Because the Senate was well along in its examination of Roberts, it could expedite the confirmation process. Roberts's sad countenance, such a contrast to the joy he had portrayed during his first nomination in July, revealed his grief over the loss of Rehnquist. "I am honored and humbled by the confidence that the president has shown in me. And I'm very much aware that if I am confirmed, I would succeed a man I deeply respect and admire, a man who has been very kind to me for twenty-five years."[14] After leaving the White House, Roberts went to the Court to serve as a pallbearer for the deceased chief.

The next week Roberts returned to Capitol Hill to begin his delayed hearings before the Senate Judiciary Committee. Seated between the senators and his family, he delivered a brief, pithy opening statement, filled with all-American references to baseball and the Mid-West landscape of his youth. He analogized the role of a judge to that of baseball umpire, calling balls and strikes as a neutral observer, never attempting to participate in the game as a pitcher or batter. Harvard-trained Roberts waxed nostalgic about his early years, like the song, "Back Home in Indiana," explaining that the endless fields of the Hoosier State represented "the limitless possibilities of our great land."[15] If confirmed as the next chief justice, he pledged to protect the laws and freedom that safeguard such endless possibilities for all Americans.

Democratic senators and moderate Republican Arlen Specter (R.-Penn.), chair of the committee, pressed him on privacy and abortion rights. The nominee agreed that the Constitution guarantees a right to privacy, but he refused to speak about specific cases, such as *Roe v. Wade*. He assured the senators, however, that he supported the doctrine of *stare decisis*, which gives deference to legal precedents. When queried about his memos expressing policy preferences during the Reagan administration, Roberts argued that he was simply advocating a position as a "staff lawyer," not expressing his own views. Liberals and moderates were skeptical, and, as the eight hours of questioning Roberts wore on over several days, some senators became frustrated and angry at his skillful parrying of their attempts to determine his views on a variety of issues. The talents that Roberts had used to help his side win twenty-five cases of the thirty-nine he had argued before the high court—poise, preparedness, gentility, fluency, and wit—helped him weather the verbal salvos without turning a hair. Republican senators were optimistic that he would ultimately be confirmed. The committee voted 13–5 to send the nomination to the full Senate, which confirmed Roberts 78–22 on September 29, 2005.

John Paul Stevens, the most senior member of the Court, in age and years of service, administered the oath of office to Roberts at the White House. When the justices ascended the bench on the first Monday in October, fifty-year-old John Roberts was now their leader in the center chair. One of his first acts as chief justice was to send staff members to John Marshall's historic home in Richmond, Virginia. Their assignment was to retrieve the great chief justice's robe, on display in the house, and return to Washington with it. Rehnquist had copied his robe after a Gilbert and Sullivan operetta character (complete with four shiny gold metallic stripes on each sleeve); Roberts wanted his robe to model the fourth chief justice's during his service from 1801 to 1835.

Anyone who attended oral argument in Chief Justice Roberts's first weeks on the bench noticed an immediate difference in his style from "the old chief," as the departed Rehnquist was now called. Though affable off the bench, Rehnquist was usually a stern taskmaster in the Court's public sessions, cutting advocates off in mid-sentence if their time expired. He once growled at a floundering attorney, "You are making this Court wonder if you are qualified to argue before it!" In contrast, Roberts is more likely to display his dry sense of humor and easy-going tone. Occasionally, he allows lawyers to run a few minutes over their allotted time.

On Halloween 2005, less than a month after he took over the Court's helm, a loud bang echoed above the bench in the middle of oral argument. It's a "trick they play on new chief justices all the time," Roberts joshed.[16] He thus diffused the tension caused by an exploding light bulb in the ceiling. Appropriately for his sense of humor, the chief dressed up as Groucho Marx for "trick or treat" at his house that night.

During the 2008 Washington, D.C., gun control case, he jokingly sparred with the advocate defending the policy requiring gun triggers to be locked: "So, if you hear an intruder in your house in the middle of the night," the chief asked, "all you have to do is turn on the light at your bedside table, put on your reading glasses [the fifty-three-year-old chief now wears half-glasses perched on his nose], and read the numbers of the combination lock on your gun?"

With his respect for the institution and his more senior colleagues (he is seven years the junior of the Court's previously youngest member, Clarence Thomas), Roberts adopted a formal approach in conducting his first conference. He called his colleagues by their titles and surnames. Because he is considered "the first among equals," the chief justice guides the discussion of cases already heard in oral argument, as well as whether to accept cases that have come to the Court on appeal. After stating his views first, a tradition in the conference which is held behind closed doors with only the justices in attendance, the chief then turned in order of seniority to "Justice Stevens," "Justice O'Connor" (who was now back at the Court because her successor had not been named), "Justice Scalia." As Roberts turned to Scalia, the voluble Italian American explained, "I will always call you Chief. But to you, I'm Nino [Scalia's nickname], and this is Sandra, and this is John."[17]

In the summer after his first term at the Court's helm, Roberts sat down for an interview with George Washington University law professor Jeffrey Rosen. They discussed at length the new chief's view of his power. "A chief justice's power is really quite limited," Roberts explained, "and the dynamic among all of the justices is going to affect whether he can accomplish much or not."[18] He admitted that his goal was to increase collegiality and unanimity among the nine justices because unanimous decisions are more difficult to overturn. More stability in the law, in turn, produces more public respect for the tribunal. Not surprisingly, in light of his "robe model," Roberts named Chief Justice John Marshall as the historical embodiment of how to lead the Court. The Marshall era is known for its unanimous decisions, most authored by the chief justice himself, with few concurring or dissenting opinions. Roberts cited Marshall's conviviality as the trait most likely to have led to his success in marshaling the Court. Any visitors to the Great Chief Justice's home in Richmond leave with that image of John Marshall. His townhouse is located in the center of the Virginia capital, near the historic statehouse designed by his distant cousin and political antagonist, Thomas Jefferson. The dining room in the home is set as often it was during Marshall's life there, when he would invite friends and neighbors for dinner, followed by Madeira. When the justices gathered in Washington for short Court sessions during the Marshall era, they lived communally in a boarding house, and the chief would similarly wine and dine his colleagues.

As Roberts's first term as chief proceeded, it seemed that his own spirit of good will was leading the Court to more unanimous decisions. A string of 9–0 rulings came down over a period of weeks. In the final days of the term, however, the justices fractured on terrorism, the death penalty, and gerrymandering. Nevertheless, the 2005–06 term reflected more unanimity (in nearly forty percent of the cases) than the final two terms of the Rehnquist era (thirty and twenty-seven percent, respectively). Roberts voted with the majority in over ninety percent of the sixty-nine cases, which meant that, by tradition, he chose the author of the Court's opinion the lion's share of the time. He self-assigned in eight instances.

In the most visible and consequential of the Court's decisions during Roberts's first term, the chief justice had to recuse himself. The D.C. Circuit ruling upholding the Bush administration's policy of using military commissions, which had come down the day of Roberts's interview at the White House, and in which he had voted with the majority, was overturned by the Supreme Court in *Hamdan v. Rumsfeld*. The very first opinion he issued on the high bench was a dissent in *Georgia v. Randolph*, which invalidated the search of a home when its co-occupant had explicitly refused to permit police entry (despite the other occupant's consent to the search). His conservative colleagues, Scalia and Thomas, sided with him. The chief's disagreement with the five-person majority was consistent with his rulings on the circuit in favor of police authority. He also sided with the government in a 5–4 decision allowing Kansas to apply the death penalty automatically if the jury finds the reasons for and against the capital sentence to be equal.

Roberts wrote for a unanimous Court in a case closely followed by universities, *Rumsfeld v. Forum for Academic and Institutional Rights*. The chief's opinion for the Court determined that the federal law requiring law schools receiving government funding to offer military recruiters the same access to their campuses as other recruiters did not violate the schools' First Amendment free speech or association rights. Some law schools had wanted to ban the military because of its discriminatory policies towards gay service members. In another free speech case, Roberts voted with the majority to uphold political speech in striking down Vermont's campaign contribution and candidate expenditure limits, which the Court saw as trouncing First Amendment rights (*Randall v. Sorrell*). Yet he was not so open to public employees' assertion of free speech guarantees. The chief justice voted with four other justices that, when such employees speak pursuant to their official duties, the First Amendment does not apply to them, and their employers may discipline them (*Garcetti v. Ceballos*).

The new chief issued the Court's opinion, again unanimously, in a religious freedom case. Roberts declared that the federal government had failed to show a compelling state interest, as required by the 1993 Religious Freedom Restoration

Act, in barring a small religious sect's liturgical use of a hallucinogenic controlled substance (*Gonzales v. O Centro Espirita BUV*).

On the issue of applying the Vienna Convention to a foreign detainee in American courts, Roberts wrote for a six-person majority that a state may apply its own procedural rules to such cases (*Sanchez-Llamas v. Oregon*). Despite the liberal dissenters' view that the Convention conferred rights on individuals that were enforceable in U.S. courts, Roberts opinion refused to resolve that larger question, an example of his desire to craft narrow rulings when possible. Two of the dissenters, Justices Breyer and Ginsburg, are more amenable to enforcing rights established by international law and treaties than are their conservative colleagues.

A closely watched redistricting case from Texas (*League of United Latin American Citizens v. Perry*) found Roberts siding with the conservative majority to approve a mid-decade, Republican-led gerrymander in the Lone Star state. When Justice Anthony Kennedy, the swing voter, abandoned that bloc, Roberts found himself in dissent from the majority's view that the Texas legislature violated the Voting Rights Act in redrawing lines that diluted a Latino voting district.

In a case that intertwined federal power and physician-assisted suicide (*Gonzales v. Oregon*), Roberts dissented with his fellow conservatives, Scalia and Thomas, from the majority's view that the Controlled Substances Act does not allow the U.S. attorney general to make medical policy decisions. Thus, he could not prohibit Oregon doctors from prescribing federally regulated drugs for use in physician-assisted suicide under a *state* law permitting the procedure.

Mid-way through the 2005–06, Justice O'Connor's replacement finally took his seat on the Court. Justice Samuel Alito joined the bench on January 31, 2006. The 2006–07 term, therefore, would be the first full session in which President George W. Bush's two appointments would sit in all of the cases. By the term's end, observers agreed that the Court had taken a turn to the right, but Roberts had fallen short of his goal to increase unanimity among his colleagues. The Court issued a new low of sixty-eight opinions, one-third of which were decided 5–4. Justice Kennedy was in the majority in each of those twenty-four rulings. Unanimity dropped to just under one-quarter of the signed opinions. The highest frequency of voting together was Roberts and Alito at nearly ninety percent.

Chief Justice Roberts issued the Court's opinion in three high-profile rulings during the term. *Morse v. Frederick* presented the question of whether public schools could punish a student for speech displayed at a school-sanctioned and school-supervised event. Frederick, a senior in high school, unfurled a sign saying "Bong Hits 4 Jesus" across the street from his Juneau, Alaska, school during a parade in honor of the Olympic torch-bearer. Students had permission to attend the parade during the school day. The student argued that the school violated his First Amendment free speech rights when Morse, the principal, asked him to take down his sign, then grabbed it away from him, and, ultimately, suspended Frederick for ten days. Roberts wrote for a five-justice majority that at a school event the school could restrict a message promoting drug abuse that conflicted with the district's policy discouraging such activities. Again writing for a 5–4 Court, the chief upheld core *political* speech by accepting a challenge to the 2002 McCain–Feingold law's restrictions on television advertising by corporations and unions (*FEC v. Wisconsin Right to Life*). His most publicized opinion of the term came down on its last day, June 28, 2007. In a dramatic announcement, Roberts declared for the five-person majority that public schools in Seattle and Louisville could not voluntarily use race to assign and bus children to schools in order to integrate them (*Parents Involved in Community Schools v. Seattle School District* and *Meredith v. Jefferson County Board of Education*). Even if the schools would resegregate without such policies, Roberts ruled that they violated the 14th Amendment's Equal Protection Clause. "The only way to stop discrimination on the basis of race," he starkly concluded, "is to stop discriminating on the basis of race."[19]

A controversial abortion case, *Gonzales v. Carhart*, found Roberts on the winning side of the narrowly split Court, upholding the federal Partial Birth Abortion Ban. The justices were similarly divided 5–4, with the chief in the majority, in ruling that taxpayers do not have standing (legal status) to bring suits challenging expenditures of federal funds to support the Bush administration's Office of Faith-Based and Community Initiatives (*Hein v. Freedom from Religion, Inc.*). The Court also stymied a law suit brought by a woman against her employer under Title VII of the 1964 Civil Rights Act. Roberts sided with the five justices who argued that the statute requires complaints claiming gender-based pay discrimination must be filed within 180 days of the incident in order to sue (*Ledbetter v. Goodyear Tire*).

In two death penalty cases, Roberts sided with the government in the Court's opinion allowing prosecutors to remove potential jurors who are ambivalent about the death penalty (*Uttecht v. Brown*) and, in dissent, from the majority view that a delusional mentally ill convicted murderer could not be executed because he lacked a "rational understanding" of why the state had imposed capital punishment on him.

Roberts, along with all the Court's members but Justice Stevens, split on police practices involving automobiles. With only Stevens in dissent, the Court sanctioned the police decision to force a speeding driver off the road, despite the subsequent wreck that left him paralyzed (*Scott v. Harris*). In a less dangerous context, however, where police stop a car, the Court ruled unanimously that a passenger has the same right, under the Fourth Amendment, as a driver to question the validity of the vehicle stop (*Brendlin v. California*).

The chief justice dissented from a ruling celebrated by environmentalists in *Massachusetts v. EPA*. The liberal majority determined that the Bay State had standing to bring suit against the EPA, which, in turn, had the legal authority under the Clean Air Act to regulate greenhouse gases emitted by cars. Roberts, typically wanting a narrow decision, asserted that Massachusetts did not have standing to bring the suit in the first place. Thus, he never would have reached the substantive issue of the EPA's authority.

Before he could preside over the opening of his third term on the high tribunal, Chief Justice Roberts faced a frightening medical challenge. Vacationing in August 2007 with his family at their summer home in Maine, he suddenly suffered a seizure and hit his head on a boat dock. He was rushed to a local hospital, where he spent forty-eight hours under observation. What the public had not known at the time of his appointment to the Court in 2005 was that he had experienced a similar episode fourteen years earlier. The cause of such episodes can range from epilepsy to stroke to brain tumors to viral infections to change in medication. The doctors found no life-threatening condition in their tests, but informed observers say that Roberts might have to take medication to lessen the chance of another seizure. Justices are under no obligation to make their medical records public.

The chief justice seemed hail and hearty at the start of the 2007–08 term, and he issued one of the Court's most anxiously awaited opinions—one that literally had life or death ramifications. Writing for a 7–2 majority, Roberts upheld Kentucky's three-drug protocol for lethal injections, which is also used by the federal government and thirty-four other states. The Court reasoned that the procedure did not risk causing such pain that it ran afoul of the Eighth Amendment's guarantee against cruel and unusual punishment (*Baze v. Rees*). The chief voted with the four-justice minority in dissent against the Court's decision declaring that Louisiana's death penalty law for child rapists was unconstitutional (*Kennedy v. Louisiana*).

Roberts's oral argument anecdote about trying to open the combination on a locked gun as an intruder enters the owner's house signaled his vote in 2008's *District of Columbia v. Heller*, where the Supreme Court, via Justice Scalia's opinion, ruled that the Second Amendment protects individual rights to gun ownership. Therefore, Washington's strict handgun ban fell victim to the five-justice majority. The chief was in dissent, however, when Justice Kennedy led the liberal members of the Court to rule that suspected terrorists incarcerated at Guantanamo Bay, Cuba, have a constitutional right to challenge their imprisonment in federal courts (*Boumediene v. Bush*).

For the second time since taking his seat on the high Court, Roberts issued an opinion thwarting international law. In 2008's *Medellin v. Texas*, the chief found for a six-justice majority that neither International Court of Justice interpretations of international treaties nor President Bush's executive orders to follow them required Texas to reopen a death penalty case involving a foreign national.

Roberts sided with the majority in upholding Indiana's law requiring voters to present government-issued picture identification in order to cast ballots (*Crawford v. Marion County Election Board*). Many observers noted that Roberts must have been pleased with the 6–3 vote in the Indiana case and the 7–2 result in the Kentucky lethal injection case. Indeed, 5–4 decisions in 2007–08 dropped by 10 (24 to 14) from the previous term, and 7–2 outcomes more than doubled (9 to 20) between the two terms. Yet unanimous 9–0 rulings have decreased (45 to 28 to 21) over the past three sessions of the Court.

Speaking at the end of the 2006–07 term to another group of teachers attending a seminar on the Court, Chief Justice Roberts quipped about the closely decided decisions handed down earlier that day: Some "might think I need to know more about the Supreme Court and constitutional law!" He encouraged the educators in their endeavors, noting, "If you are not able to teach your students about the Court effectively, its role will be diminished. I know you have a challenging task." Turning whimsical again, he teased, "Looking around the room at the [dour] portraits of the first eight chief justices, I'm struck that they not have been the most inspiring teachers!"[20] Whether John Roberts will be "great" chief justice, like his role model John Marshall, remains to be seen. But his charming, self-deprecating wit, combined with his sparkling intellect, have already made him an inspiration.

CHAPTER TWO

John Paul Stevens

A visitor to Justice John Paul Stevens's chambers at the U.S. Supreme Court is likely to find him dressed informally in a short-sleeved sport shirt, open at the collar. His mode of dress matches his demeanor—unpretentious, modest, welcoming. On the bench, he sports his trademark bow tie, and, with his silver-white hair combed straight back, the eighty-eight-year-old associate justice with the warm smile looks like everyone's favorite grandfather. As Stevens speaks in oral argument, his flat, Midwestern accent reveals his Illinois roots, and his respectful, yet keenly incisive, questions posed to attorneys appearing before the Court demonstrate the brilliant intellect that has marked his academic and professional pursuits.

Born April 20, 1920, in Chicago, Stevens was the youngest of Ernest James Stevens and Elizabeth Street Stevens's four sons. Elizabeth was an English teacher, and Ernest acquired considerable wealth in the hotel and insurance businesses. His father established and managed the 3,000-room Stevens Hotel, which is now the stately Chicago Hilton on Michigan Avenue. At the hotel young John met a parade of notables, including celebrated aviators Charles Lindbergh and Amelia Earhart. The prominent Stevens family lived in the then-grand neighborhood surrounding the University of Chicago, and John received his elementary and preparatory education at the university's Laboratory School. It obviously prepared him well, for he went on to graduate from the University of Chicago in 1941 *magna cum laude*, Phi Beta Kappa, and first in his class. At the university, he had majored in English, edited the student newspaper, and joined Psi Upsilon, the fraternity his father had pledged at Chicago. Fresh out of college, Stevens married his childhood sweetheart Elizabeth Jane Sheeran in 1942; their marriage lasted thirty-seven years and produced four children (John, Kathryn, Elizabeth, and Susan). The Stevens were divorced in 1979, and Justice Stevens married Maryan Mulholland Simon shortly thereafter. Son John succumbed to cancer in 1996.

Like most men of his generation, Stevens entered the military during World War II. From 1942 to 1945 he served in the United States Navy as a watch officer, analyzing and breaking the code of intercepted Japanese communications at Pearl Harbor after the infamous attack there. For service in the Communications Intelligence Organization, which led the U.S. to shoot down the plane of Japanese Navy commander Admiral Isoroku Yamamoto, Stevens was awarded the Bronze Star.

Before the war, Stevens had considered following in his mother's footsteps by becoming a teacher, but one of his older brothers, an attorney, encouraged him to pursue a degree at Northwestern University Law School, which their father had attended. Perhaps witnessing his father's unjust conviction (later overturned) for embezzling funds from the family's insurance company when the Stevens Hotel went bankrupt in 1934 also directed John toward the law.

Duplicating his undergraduate success, John Stevens earned the highest grades in the law school's history, became editor of the law review, graduated first in his class and *magna cum laude*, and was elected to the Order of the Coif law honorary. After graduating from law school in 1947, Stevens continued on the most prestigious course in the law profession, serving a U.S. Supreme Court clerkship. From October 1947 to July 1948 he clerked for Justice Wiley Rutledge, a Franklin Roosevelt appointee and distinguished civil libertarian who, like Stevens, hailed from the Midwest. To this day, Stevens names Rutledge among his judicial heroes, along with Chief Justice John Marshall and Justices Louis Brandeis, Oliver Wendell Holmes, and Benjamin Cardozo.

Admitted to the Illinois bar in 1949, Stevens returned to his hometown to take a position at the leading Chicago law firm of Poppenhusen, Johnston, Thompson, and Raymond. He served as an associate there for three years, developing a well-regarded expertise in antitrust law. He also lectured on the subject at Northwestern and eventually at the University of Chicago law schools. In 1951 the future justice served as associate counsel for the U.S. House of Representatives' Subcommittee on the Study of Monopoly Power. He then became a named partner in his own firm of Rothschild, Stevens, Barry, and Myers, established in the early 1950s. While a partner there, Stevens also served as a member of the U.S. Attorney General's National Committee to Study the Antitrust Laws from 1953 to 1955. His reputation as a superb attorney of notable integrity spread, and in 1969 the Illinois Supreme Court appointed him chief counsel to a special commission investigating judicial impropriety among state judges. Observing that one of the state's Supreme Court justices withdrew his dissent from the decision that tarred the Illinois court with the brush of corruption, Stevens vowed to speak his mind in dissenting and concurring opinions after he joined the federal bench.

The commission's work generated intense public scrutiny and brought Stevens's name to prominence. Based on the publicity, Senator Charles Percy (R.-Ill.) called John Stevens to his office and told him that he would like to suggest his name for the U.S. Court of Appeals for the Seventh Circuit. Percy and Stevens were college friends who had lost touch, and the Illinois senator seemed unaware of their past association when he met with Stevens in 1969. Percy asked Stevens about his party affiliation, saying it would be easier if he were a Republican. Stevens replied that he came from a Republican family (his father had supported President Warren G. Garding) but had never run for office, so his partisan label was not public knowledge.[1] Earl Pollock, a prominent Chicago antitrust lawyer, once described Stevens as "almost a nonpolitical animal."[2] In 1970 President Richard Nixon nominated John Paul Stevens to his first judgeship, a position on the Seventh Circuit Court of Appeals.

Judge Stevens's tenure on the Court of Appeals produced approximately 200 opinions that were lengthy and filled with footnotes, reflecting his precise and detailed approach to the law. In substance, they were considered pragmatic, moderate, and imaginative. A body of Stevens's opinions that represented more conservative views caught the attention of President Gerald Ford's administration as they searched for a nominee to replace Justice William O. Douglas when ill health forced him to retire in 1975. On the circuit bench, for example, Stevens pragmatically argued in favor of a dress code for public school teachers—not because he valued uniformity over individualism, but because he believed "that each choice between conformity and diversity is itself affected by a variety of factors, and local school boards need the freedom to make diverse choices for themselves."[3] Stevens has always been skeptical of broad judge-made formulas that limit the application of relevant facts in future cases.

The president's wife, Betty Ford, who became an outspoken advocate of women's causes during her husband's brief tenure as president after Nixon resigned in 1974, put public pressure on President Ford to name the first woman to the U.S. Supreme Court. The president consulted with Attorney General Edward H. Levi and White House Counsel Philip Buchen, requesting that they draft a list of potential nominees, and specifically instructing them to include female candidates. Ford then submitted an initial list to the American Bar Association's Committee on Judiciary for a preliminary review. They declared the list "a good one, which was responsibly drawn." It contained the names of two members of Congress and five federal circuit court judges, including Stevens, but no female candidates. The administration submitted a second list of possible nominees, including two women circuit judges. The final choice narrowed to two candidates: Judge Stevens and Judge Arlin M. Adams of the Third Circuit Court of Appeals, who had appeared on the initial list; Ford chose the former after a final consultation with Levi and Buchen. (Levi had asked Stevens to lecture at the University of Chicago when Levi was dean of the law school there.)

Stevens recalls that he had met President Ford for the first time only a few days before the nomination. The occasion was a White House dinner for the federal judiciary, where Stevens chatted with Ford over drinks and during the post-dinner dance when Ford circulated to Stevens's table. They discussed the New York City debt crisis and whether the federal government should bail out the Big Apple. Although Ford exhibited no special interest in Stevens that night, the president called him at the end of the week with the stunning news of his nomination. Typically modest in his assessment of the factors leading to his appointment, Stevens simply avows that he was a "noncontroversial, Midwestern, appellate court judge."[4] The lack of controversy that marked Stevens and his career was indeed determinative. Chief Justice Warren Burger wanted to expedite the process of filling the seat vacated by Douglas in the middle of the 1975–76 term after months of absence due to his long illness. Moreover, the White House desired a smooth confirmation to place Ford's nominee on the Supreme Court *before* the 1976 presidential election in case Ford lost (which, of course, he did; the winner, Jimmy Carter, had no opportunities to nominate a justice to the high bench during his four-year term).

In announcing Stevens's nomination to the public on November 28, 1975, Ford called the circuit court judge "the best qualified [candidate]. . . . Judge Stevens is held in the highest esteem by his colleagues in the legal profession and the judiciary and has had an outstanding career in the practice and teaching of law as well as on the federal bench."[5] After a thorough analysis of his circuit court opinions, the ABA's committee rated Stevens "highly qualified" by virtue of his "high standards of professional competence, judicial temperament and integrity." Awarding their highest evaluation to Stevens, the ABA panel announced that Stevens's lower- court opinions "show a uniformly high degree of scholarship, discipline, and conscientiousness."[6]

During the three days of hearings before the Senate Judiciary Committee, Judge Stevens asserted that he would follow the same policy of "judicial restraint" on the Supreme Court that he had adhered to on the court of appeals, where his opinions demonstrated respect for established procedures rather than for any particular ideology. He commented, "It's always been my philosophy to decide cases on the narrowest grounds possible and not to reach out."[7] Describing the role of a judge, Stevens argued before the Judiciary Committee that jurists did not "have a charter" to substitute their own views for the law. Judges should confine themselves to "deciding no more than the specific controversy" presented by the case before them. He predicted that he would be "most reluctant to depart from prior precedent without a clear showing" that a departure was necessary. Although Stevens noted that he placed a "very high value on the First Amendment," he admitted that "there are occasions when restrictions [on the press] are justified by national security," such as in the reporting of troop movements.[8] At a time when the states were debating the Equal Rights Amendment, Stevens maintained that amending the Constitution should be eschewed when legislation could achieve the same goals sought by the constitutional change. Predictably, women's groups advocating passage of the ERA criticized Stevens's nomination. Nevertheless, the Judiciary Committee approved him by a vote of 13-0, and sent his name to the full Senate, which confirmed him within a week by the unanimous vote of 98-0.

Stevens's confirmation, coming just sixteen days after President Ford officially submitted his name to the Senate for its constitutionally mandated role to "advise and consent," was one of the fastest for any of the justices then sitting on the Supreme Court. It would be among the last in the final quarter of the twentieth century to sail so smoothly through the nomination and appointment process. On December 19, 1975, John Paul Stevens, at age fifty-five, took the oath of office to assume the ninth seat on the Supreme Court.

Looking back over his more than three decades on the nation's highest court, Justice Stevens recalls that he felt at home from his earliest days there. "I wasn't a stranger here, and I did feel that my background and memories as a clerk [to Justice Rutledge] brought a lot of practices and customs of the Court back to mind. . . . Also, my experience as a law clerk is the reason I didn't join the pool (in which one clerk from each chamber prepares a shared memo on each of the [9,000] . . . petitions for writs of *certiorari* [asking the Court to hear the case on appeal]. I had some familiarity with cert work, and I thought I could get through the [petitions] faster without joining the pool. And that opinion hasn't changed."[9] He remains the only justice outside the "cert pool."

Upon Stevens's 1975 nomination to the Supreme Court, the press noted that he was neither a partisan nor an ideologue. His record on the high court over his thirty-two-year tenure (and closing in on the record thirty-six-and-a-half year service of his predecessor Justice Douglas) has defied simplistic classification. He still considers himself a conservative judge who hews to precedent and submerges his own policy predelections in favor of processes established in the American democratic system. To those observers who label him a liberal, he responds that he has not moved left on the spectrum. Rather, he argues, the Court's ideological center has shifted with the appointments of increasingly conservative justices.

In terms of opinion production, Stevens's first four months on the Court were illustrative; he was the most prolific opinion writer among his colleagues. Whereas freshmen justices typically maintain a low profile, Stevens wrote nine opinions, including four dissents from conservative majority opinions in the first half of his initial term on the high tribunal. Now as the Court's most senior justice in age and time of service, he proclaims, "I just feel I have an obligation to expose my views to the public."[10] Stevens continues his prolific opinion output, even as the Supreme Court's decisions fall to record low numbers below 70 cases per term. In 2007–08 the tribunal's oldest member authored the most opinions (31), consisting of 6 majority, 1 plurality, 10 concurrences, and 14 dissents. Statistics reflect his influence on decision outcomes. In the more than 3,300 cases resulting in opinions or judgments in which he has participated during his thirty-two years on the high court, Stevens has been in the majority nearly three-quarters of the time.

His early voting patterns pleasantly surprised civil libertarians. Women's rights groups that had feared that Stevens was insensitive to gender discrimination commended him after his first two terms on the Court for his votes and opinions favoring civil rights for women. In the term ending in June 1977, Stevens sided with the Court's staunchest liberals (Justices William Brennan and Thurgood Marshall) nearly 60 percent of the time. Three decades later, over two-thirds of his more than 3,000 opinions that can be labelled ideologically reflect a liberal stance. He now agrees most often with liberal Justices Ruth Bader Ginsburg, David Souter, and Stephen Breyer, ranging from 79 percent to 67 percent, respectively, in the 2006-07 term. Conversely, his agreement with conservative colleagues Samuel Alito, John Roberts, Antonin Scalia, and Clarence Thomas, ran in the same term, respectively, from a high of 42 percent to a low of 32 percent.

In women's rights cases, Justice Stevens has typically voted on the side upholding the cause of gender equity. The 1976 *General Electric Co. v. Gilbert* case found him in dissent (along with Brennan and Marshall) from the Court's opinion that a private employer's disability plan excluding pregnancy from coverage is not invidiously discriminatory. The three dissenters were vindicated when Congress overturned the Court's ruling with legislation. In another 1976 decision, *Craig v. Boren*, Stevens was with the majority in voting to strike down an Oklahoma law that banned the sale of "3.2 beer" to men under twenty-one but allowed sales to women over eighteen. Stevens joined Justices Brennan, Marshall, and Byron White in dissenting from the Court's Rehnquist-led majority, which upheld California's statutory rape law punishing males, but not females, for sexual intercourse with an underage partner of the opposite sex. The Supreme Court in *Michael M. v. Superior Court* deemed the disparate treatment of men and women not irrational because "only women may become pregnant." Again voting in dissent, Stevens disagreed with the 2007 majority in *Ledbetter v. Goodyear Tire*, which ruled that a woman could not sue her employer under Title VII of the 1964 Civil Rights Act for alleged gender-based pay discrimination that has occurred throughout her career. Justice Alito, writing for the 5–4 majority, argued that the law required plaintiffs to bring their suits within 180 days after a discrete instance of alleged bias.

Justice Stevens has maintained a consistent pro-choice position in the contentious abortion litigation that has come before the Court. He dissented from the Court's energized conservative faction in 1989 when it upheld Missouri's attempts to limit abortions in *Webster v. Reproductive Health Services*. He would have gone a step further than the controlling plurality in 1992's *Planned Parenthood of Southeastern Pennsylvania v. Casey*, which upheld abortion as a fundamental right, to reaffirm the trimester system of *Roe v. Wade* that had allowed virtually unlimited access to abortions in the first three months of pregnancy. The *Casey* plurality, consisting of Justices Anthony Kennedy, Souter, and Sandra Day O'Connor, approved state limits on abortion unless they constituted an "undue burden" on a woman seeking the procedure.

In 2007 Stevens told Jeffrey Rosen that Justice Harry Blackmun's opinion for the 7–2 majority in Roe, two years before Stevens joined the Court, contained unnecessarily convoluted reasoning. Stevens believes that Justice Potter Stewart's succinct position that marital and family privacy, established by the Court in a 1965 precedent (*Griswold v. Connecticut*), encompassed a woman's right to abortion. Justice Stevens has voted twice to invalidate bans on so-called partial-birth abortions. He was with the majority to strike down a state prohibition in the 2000 case of *Stenberg v. Carhart*, but in the minority to do the same for a federal proscription in 2007's *Gonzales v. Carhart*. Justice O'Connor's replacement with more conservative Justice Alito swung the 5–4 Court from invalidating such bans to approving them.

Civil rights issues involving race are more typical of Stevens's case-by-case analysis of constitutional and statutory interpretation. He disappointed affirmative action proponents by his vote in the landmark *Bakke* case to invalidate the University of California at Davis Medical School's quota system for admitting minorities. (Justice Lewis Powell's controlling opinion struck down the use of quotas but upheld the balance of the affirmative action program, with race to be used as a "plus" factor in admissions.) Stevens abstained from voting in the 1979 *Weber* case, in which Justice Brennan upheld a private employer's affirmative action plan over the challenge from a white worker who had been excluded from an apprentice training program solely based on race. The next year Stevens dissented in *Fullilove v. Klutznick* from the majority's ruling in favor of Congress's 10-percent set-aside quota for "minority business enterprises" in federal construction contracts. Stevens's angry dissent, which he read from the bench the day the decision came down, labelled the set-aside law "perverse" and compared it to the Nazi laws that defined who was a Jew. He now admits, "I think my rhetoric was probably a little strong,"[11] but he still believes his dissent was correct.

Justice Stevens continued to vote against minority racial preferences until 1986–87, when he joined the Court's liberal faction (consisting of Justices Brennan, Marshall, Blackmun, and sometimes Powell) to support affirmative action programs then under attack by the Reagan administration. In 1989 Stevens reverted to his *Fullilove* position, however, in joining the conservative justices in *Croson* to strike down a *local* set-aside quota that required 30 percent of Richmond, Virginia, construction contracts to be let to minority-owned companies. The very next year, Stevens switched sides again, this time in *Metro Broadcasting v. Federal Communications Commission.* Following Justice Brennan's leadership in his last opinion before retirement, Stevens voted to *uphold* the FCC's affirmative action policy to increase minority ownership of broadcast licenses. Revealing his fact-based approach to cases, Stevens argued in his brief concurring opinion that *Fullilove* differed from *Metro Broadcasting* because the latter concerned an area (broadcasting) where racial and ethnic characteristics are truly relevant.

How would the mercurial Stevens vote in 1995's *Adarand Constructors v. Peña,* which again challenged federal set-aside programs? If he held to his positions in *Fullilove* and *Croson,* he would vote to invalidate the program. Yet he was more recently on record as supporting the minority-preference scheme in *Metro Broadcasting.* Although Justices Scalia and Thomas wanted to strike down *all* such racial classifications, Justice O'Connor's opinion for the Court in *Adarand* argued that such classifications could survive "strict scrutiny" (the highest level of judicial examination under the Fourteenth Amendment's Equal Protection Clause) *if* the government could prove a compelling state interest in classifying on the basis of race. O'Connor declared that a general policy of "racial diversity" could not meet the "compelling" test. Her decision also explicitly overruled the *Metro Broadcasting* precedent and declared *Fullilove* to be no longer controlling. Justice Stevens (the senior associate justice among the dissenters, which included Justices Souter, Ginsburg, and Breyer) wrote the lead dissent, urging adherence to precedent, including *Fullilove*; distinction between *federal* set-aside programs (justifiable) and *state* set-aside mandates (unjustifiable); and recognition of "invidious" discrimination in the workplace, in contrast to efforts at merely promoting "diversity."

Yet Stevens shifted from his *Bakke* position to vote with the O'Connor-led majority that upheld the University of Michigan Law School's affirmative action policy, using race as a "plus" to create a diverse student body. The 2003 *Grutter v. Bollinger* landmark ruling agreed with Powell's reasoning in *Bakke* that diversity in education is a compelling state interest that allows the use of racial classifications, as long as they are narrowly tailored to meet the state's goal. In the companion case, *Gratz v. Bollinger*, Stevens dissented from the conservative majority, which included O'Connor, in its finding that the University of Michigan undergraduate college's 20-point bonus awarded to underrepresented minority applicants failed the narrow-tailoring test. His dissenting opinion, however, focused on the procedural fact that Gratz, a white woman denied admission to UM, had already graduated from another institution and, therefore, did not have legal standing to bring the lawsuit. When race in education returned to the justices in two cases (*Parents Involved in Community Schools v. Seattle School District No. 1* and *Meredith v. Jefferson County Board of Education*) involving its use in K–12 public school assignments, Stevens produced a testy dissent from the bare majority invalidating the policy.

Civil rights advocates also had reason to cheer Stevens in the 1990's cases challenging so-called majority-minority voting districts. While the more conservative bloc on the high court took a skeptical view toward bizarrely shaped districts drawn with race as the predominant criterion, Stevens joined the liberal bloc in dissent, arguing that race-based districts are necessary to ensure fair representation of minorities in Congress and state legislatures.

In First Amendment free expression and free press cases, Stevens has applied his patented nondoctrinaire analysis. Among his first decisions for the Court in this realm was his majority opinion in *Federal Communications Commission v. Pacifica Foundation.* The 1978 case arose out of litigation over a complaint lodged with the FCC by a father who, while driving with his young son, inadvertently tuned his car radio to a monologue by comedian George Carlin on the "seven dirty words" that cannot be used on television. To the father's shock and embarrassment, Carlin articulated each word in the septet, none of which a parent would want his young child to hear or repeat. The FCC agreed with the complaint and prohibited radio transmission of such "offensive—indecent but not obscene—words" during so-called "family hours." Stevens, writing the majority opinion for himself, Chief Justice Warren Burger and Justices Powell, Blackmun, and Rehnquist, upheld the FCC's decision. He noted that words "patently, offensively, referring to excretory and sexual organs and activities" could be banned from radio broadcasts, which intrude upon "the privacy of the home [or car], where the individual's right to be left alone plainly outweighs the First Amendment rights of an intruder."[12] The words at issue were not in a book or theater production that an adult had voluntarily chosen to view.

The distinction between willful and inadvertent exposure to material was dispositive for Stevens in writing the majority's 1997 opinion striking down the Communications Decency Act, which marked Congress's attempt to protect minors from "indecent" and "patently offensive" communications on the Internet. Though the oldest member of the Court, Stevens was among the first justices to embrace word processing, and he drafts opinions at his computer keyboard. He declared that the "odds are slim" that a user would enter a sexually explicit site by accident. He thus distinguished Websites from radio or television broadcasts, which could bombard an unsuspecting listener or viewer. In contrast, "the Internet requires a series of affirmative steps more deliberate and directed than merely turning a dial." Stevens concluded for the Court in *Reno v. American Civil Liberties Union* that "[n]otwithstanding the legitimacy and importance of the congressional goal of protecting children from harmful materials . . . the statute abridges 'the freedom of speech' protected by the First Amendment."[13] He also voted with the majority in 2002 to void, as a First Amendment violation, the 1996 Child Pornography Prevention Act. The federal law had criminalized the creation, distribution, or possession of "virtual child pornography" produced by computer images that did not depict real children. Yet six years later, in *United States v. Williams,* Stevens joined six other justices in voting to uphold Congress's more narrowly tailored criminalization of "pandering" real, purportedly obscene child porn.

On another emotive issue, flag-burning as a form of political protest, Stevens voted twice (in 1989's *Texas v. Johnson* and 1990's *U.S. v. Eichman*) to uphold flag-protection legislation at both the state and federal levels. Each time, he dissented with Chief Justice Rehnquist and Justices White and O'Connor, arguing that burning an American flag as a symbolic protest was *not* a form of expression protected by the First Amendment's free *speech* guarantee.

Nevertheless, beyond indecent/obscene speech and flag-burning, Stevens has been a visible advocate for free expression rights. He dissented from the Court's decision upholding a ban against abortion advice by federally funded family planning clinics in *Rust v. Sullivan*; wrote the opinion for a unanimous decision in *City of Ladue v. Gilleo*, invalidating a local ordinance banning all yard signs except ten specified types (including realtors' signs); voted with the rest of the Court in *Rubin v. Coors Brewing Co.* to strike down the Federal Alcohol Administration Act's prohibition against advertising alcohol content on beer; wrote for the Court's unanimous invalidation of Rhode Island's ban on advertising liquor prices in *44 Liquormart v. Rhode Island*; and issued a dissent from the Court's decision in *Morse v. Frederick* to reject a high school student's suit against his principal who tore down his sign "Bong Hits 4 Jesus" across the street from the school during a public parade. In his *Morse* dissent, the octogenarian justice cited the futility of Prohibition during his childhood, when his father could not serve alcohol to patrons of the Stevens Hotel. They then went to Chicago speakeasies to consume illegal gin. Stevens compared the failed policy to the anti-drug stance that caused Frederick's principal to remove his sign and suspend him for ten days.

Under the First Amendment's Establishment Clause, Stevens has supported a high wall between church and state, as demonstrated by his *Wallace v. Jaffree* opinion for the Supreme Court in 1985, striking down Alabama's statute authorizing a one-minute period of silence in all public schools "for meditation or prayer," and his vote with Justices Kennedy, Blackmun, O'Connor, and Souter declaring nonsectarian prayers at public school graduations in violation of Amendment I. In 2000 Stevens wrote the majority opinion in *Sante Fe Independent School District v. Doe* that a Texas public school's policy of choosing students to read prayers over the public address system at high school football games violated the Establishment Clause. He thus helped to hold the last line against creeping disassembling of Jefferson's wall, which remains intact only against organized school prayer. In contrast, his opposition to publicly funded vouchers that parents could use to send their children to church-sponsored schools, contested in 2002's *Zelman v. Simmons-Harris*, could not withstand the conservative majority's approval

of such funding. Stevens also held firm against displays of the Ten Commandments on government property, voting with the majority to require their removal
from two Kentucky county courthouses (*McCreary County v. American Civil Liberties
Union*), and dissenting from the ruling that allowed their display on the grounds
of the Texas state capitol (*Van Orden v. Perry*).

Stevens has been less reliable in upholding individual or group free-exercise-
of-religion claims. He voted with the majority in the notable *Oregon v. Smith* case
to uphold the state's controlled-substances ban that "incidentally" interferred with
Native Americans' liturgical use of peyote, a hallucinogenic drug. He sided with
the majority striking down the Religious Freedom Restoration Act in 1997's *City
of Boerne v. Flores*. RFRA had been Congress's effort to overturn the *Smith* decision
by resurrecting the "compelling state interest" test to void laws that infringe, even
incidentally, on religious exercises. When the city of Hialeah, Florida, banned
animal sacrifices, however, Justice Stevens followed his unanimous colleagues in
Church of the Lukumi Babalu Aye v. Hialeah, the 1993 ruling that declared the
ordinance unconstitutional because it was clearly aimed at the Cuban American
sect that sacrificed animals as part of their liturgy.

As his colleagues aged and postponed retirement, Stevens remained in the
most junior position on the bench for his first six years on the high court. (Justice
O'Connor would finally break the nomination hiatus with her landmark appointment in 1981.) Stevens's persistent junior status and his frequently idiosyncratic perception of the law combined to dilute his impact on American
jurisprudence. When Justice Blackmun retired in 1994, however, Stevens became
the most senior justice, allowing him to write the majority opinion or assign it to
a colleague if the chief justice was in dissent. Over the past decade and a half, he
has written a number of majority opinions that have garnered headlines.

In 2005 Stevens sparked a grassroots uproar when he ruled for a 5–4 Court
in *Kelo v. New London* that the Fifth Amendment's public use requirement does
not forbid a city's taking of private property, in this case a woman's home, for the
purpose of "economic development" that will increase tax revenues and improve
the local economy. Irate home owners across the nation flocked to their state
legislatures to urge passing of laws forbidding city governments from taking
private property under their eminent domain power.

Periodically, Stevens has ruled to check presidential prerogatives. His aston-
ishingly unanimous 1997 decision in the *Clinton v. Jones* case asserted that
President Bill Clinton was *not* entitled to immunity from Paula Jones's sexual
harassment suit for advances she alleged he made toward her while Arkansas's

governor. To this day Stevens believes that the Court ruled correctly, even though its decision indirectly led to independent counsel Kenneth Starr's investigation of the president and Clinton's impeachment for lying under oath.

Even more far reaching has been Stevens's opinion countering the administration of George W. Bush's approach to fighting the war on terror in the wake of al-Qaeda's September 11, 2001 attacks on the United States. In 2004's *Rasul v. Bush* Stevens issued the Court's majority ruling asserting the authority of federal courts to determine the legality of the president's indefinite detention of non-Amercian terror suspects captured abroad and held in custody at the U.S. Naval Base in Guantanamo Bay, Cuba. Stevens voted with the five-justice majority four years later in *Boumediene v. Bush* to invalidate the president and Congress's substitution of military tribunals for access to federal courts in trying "Gitmo" detainees.

Justice Stevens's decisions in favor of the federal government's authority have also made headlines. In 1995 he ruled for a narrowly divided Court in striking down *state* term limits for members of Congress in *U.S. Term Limits, Inc. v. Thornton*. He argued that such limits, which nearly half of the states had adopted, violated the constitutionally mandated uniformity of the federal system. He thus sided with the dissenters in 1997 against the majority's view in *Printz v. U.S.* that struck down several of the federally required gun-control provisions of the Brady Act. (He supported, in a losing cause, Washington, D.C.'s strict gun control laws, in the 2008 *Heller* case.) Stevens upheld Congress's authority under its interstate commerce power to regulate marijuana through the Controlled Substances Act. *Gonzales v. Raich*, in 2005, ruled that the federal government could regulate even locally cultivated marijuana for purported personal medical use despite California's law legalizing such use.

When Stevens is on the losing side of a case, he follows the tradition of assigning the lead dissent as the most senior justice if the chief justice is in the majority. "I think I've made some awfully good assignments, to tell you the truth, in dissents," he told law professor Jeffrey Rosen, citing Ginsburg's stinging criticisms of the majority in the 2007 abortion and gender discrimination cases. Stating the obvious, he oberved, "I'd rather assign majorities than dissents."[14] In so doing, he has worked to attract and maintain Justice Kennedy's swing vote on the liberal side in order to win in 5–4 decisions. In *Lawrence v. Texas*, invalidating state sodomy laws in 2003, Stevens gave Kennedy the majority opinion assignment and has praised the product "Tony" wrote in the controversial ruling that gay rights advocates applauded. Stevens authored the 2007 *Massachusetts v.*

Environmental Protection Agency decision, giving the state standing to sue the EPA for failure to regulate global warming under the Clean Air Act, with Kennedy's position in mind.

Nevertheless, Stevens's penchant for writing concurring and dissenting opinions (he has authored more than any of his colleagues and probably more than most of them combined) preserves his independent role on the Supreme Court. Just when it seems that he has crossed over the center line and joined the liberal bloc for good, he veers back toward his self-perception as a judicial conservative. Despite casting one of the only two dissenting votes (Ginsburg was the other) in *Bush v. Gore* that saw no reason to stop Florida's recount of contested votes in the 2000 presidential election, Stevens wrote for a six-justice majority to uphold Indiana's law requiring voters to present photo identification. Democrats, who had lauded his vote in *Bush v. Gore*, now chastised his 2008 opinion that Indiana's policy would not disproportionately affect poor, elderly, or handicapped voters who might not possess valid IDs. Stevens death penalty jurisprudence compelled his majority opinion outlawing the death penalty for the mentally retarded in *Atkins v. Virginia*. Three years later, in 2005, he sided with the majority to ban the use of capital punishment for juvenile offenders under eighteen. During oral argument of *Baze v. Reez*, the 2008 case that tested whether lethal injection violated the Eighth Amendment's prohibition against cruel and unusual punishment, Stevens seemingly searched for a way to vote against the sometimes excrutiatingly painful three-drug protocol used by Kentucky, thirty-four other states, and the federal government in lethal injections. Yet the facts must not have persuaded his head to go where his heart wanted to take him, and he voted with the seven-person majority that lethal injections passed constitutional muster.

Long after most individuals his age have entered retirement, Stevens gives no indication of leaving the Court (as of 2008). As long as he can still produce the first draft of his opinions, he tells his clerks, he will stay in the job he truly enjoys. In one way, he already has the perks of retirement, spending Court recesses at his condo in Ft. Lauderdale, Florida, where he loves to swim, golf, and play tennis. He continues to be an active participant in oral arguments, aways maintaining his self-effacing, considerate attitude toward counsel appearing before the imposing high tribunal. Yet his respectful demeanor belies his unique perspective on cases. As Stevens explains his role in the public work of the Court: "You have a point in mind that you think may not have been brought out . . . but you want to be sure your colleagues don't overlook that so . . . you'll ask a question to bring it out, and you're not necessarily trying to sell everybody on the position, but you want everybody to have at least the point in mind."[15]

John Paul Stevens seems to have found the perfect balance in his personal and professional life. As he closes in on two Court records, length of time on the bench and longevity of its members (Holmes was ninety when he retired), he still relishes the part of the judicial maverick. But, as the most senior justice, he more recently embraces the task of coalition builder. A "judge's judge," Stevens already knows that he wants his legacy to reside in his judicial products. "I just hope people will make their judgments based on what my written opinions say, and not on what people say they say. There's a long record there, and an awful lot of words. I just hope they say he did the best he could."[16]

CHAPTER THREE

Antonin Scalia

On a judicial bench that may be the wittiest and most lively in the Court's history, Antonin Scalia is the "King of Comedy." He can toss out one-liners and sardonic quips with the ease of a Las Vegas headliner. His use of them in judicial opinions and at oral argument is now legendary. To a struggling counsel at one of the Court's sessions, he posed a hypothetical set of facts to see how the attorney's argument might apply. The stumped lawyer paused and then, grasping at rhetorical straws, weakly replied, "Your honor, that's not the case before us." Scalia went for the punch line: "No!" he stage-whispered from the bench in mock astonishment. Of course, it wasn't the case at issue, Scalia admitted, but he wanted a response based on the hypothetical he had created. To an interviewer who requested some time with Scalia to discuss his appointment to the Supreme Court and the role his religion might have played in the process, he graciously agreed to discuss the general concept of the so-called "Catholic seat" but added parenthetically, "if that's what I sit in." A lawyer once recognized Justice Scalia pedaling next to him on an exercise bike at a Washington health club. He summoned his courage to enquire, "Excuse me. Are you Justice Scalia?" To which the burly justice replied with a smile, "No, he's thinner than I am." People beyond the Beltway are not immune from the justice's wit. Traveling out West with his family some years ago, he came upon a desk clerk at a motel who, when he saw the name on the credit card, asked if it was pronounced the same as that of the man on the Supreme Court. The justice later reported that he was tempted to reply, "How many Antonin Scalias are there?" For the record, he will tell you that his surname is pronounced, "Skuh-LEE-yuh." To his friends, he goes by the nickname "Nino."

Scalia's facility with language and witticisms may be traceable to a childhood spent with his college professor father and schoolteacher mother. S. Eugene Scalia, the justice's father, was a Sicilian-born immigrant to the United States who ultimately became a professor of Romance languages at Brooklyn College after earning a Ph.D. at Columbia. He was deeply devoted to his Roman Catholic religion and staunchly committed to analyzing literature in its original language. Translations of the Italian classics were anathema to him; texts must be read literally to avoid destroying their unique meanings. One scholar has even argued that the elder Scalia's beliefs may have shaped Justice Scalia's devotion to literal constitutional interpretation.[1]

Eugene Scalia married first-generation Italian American Catherine Panaro, and they had their only child, Antonin, on March 11, 1936, in Trenton, New Jersey. She was a college-educated elementary school teacher, whose brother Vince became a county prosecutor and role model for her young son. The Scalias lived with the Panaros until they moved to Elmhurst, New York, in Queens, where Antonin attended primary school P.S. 13 and was a model student in his middle-class Irish and Italian community. Recently, he made a nostalgic pilgrimage back to his Queens neighborhood and his grade school for a segment on CBS's *60 Minutes*. On camera, correspondent Leslie Stahl summarized his school records, noting that he was never absent, never tardy, and never scored below an A.

The next major influence on Scalia's life was his education at St. Francis Xavier, a Jesuit military prep school in lower Manhattan. His abundant intellectual and extracurricular talents were already apparent. He played the French horn, became leader of the marching band, participated on the rifle team, and landed the lead role in the school's production of *Macbeth*. One high school friend commented, "People just competed for second, he was so superior academically."[2] His lifelong conservatism was also making itself evident. A former classmate remembers that Scalia "was a conservative when he was seventeen years old. An archconservative Catholic. He could have been a member of the Curia [the governing body of the Roman Catholic Church]. He was brilliant, way above everybody else."[3] His upbringing in strict pre-Vatican II Roman Catholicism may have also influenced his pronounced adherence to legalisms in the secular world.[4] When asked if he ever considered the priesthood, Scalia recalls with a smile, "I gave that some thought and decided He wasn't calling me."[5]

Reinforcing the secondary school religious training was his undergraduate work at Georgetown University, the preeminent Jesuit institution of higher learning in the United States. His studies have been described as similar to a classical European education. All told, the future justice had six years of Latin and five years of Greek. Just as he had done in high school, young Scalia graduated first in his class and valedictorian from Georgetown in 1957 and received his history degree *summa cum laude*.

restraint + neutrality

rd behind him, he was accepted at Harvard Law
editor of the *Harvard Law Review*. In the late
till influenced by the judicial philosophy of Felix
r there, who had been appointed to the Supreme
1939. The Frankfurtian approach to constitu-
dicial restraint and adherence to neutral princi-
ld embrace in his own jurisprudence.[6] Again,
to his contemporaries. One of his fellow officers
calia would express his doubts over how much
government could do to help people. In 1960 he received his law degree *magna
cum laude* and earned a Sheldon Fellowship for postgraduate study and travel in
Europe.

While at Harvard, Scalia had met and become engaged to Radcliffe undergraduate Maureen McCarthy. They were married in September 1960. His parents
considered it a "mixed marriage" because she was *Irish* Catholic. By 1962 they
started their family, which grew to nine children over the next nineteen years. By
all accounts, theirs has been a strong union sealed by their mutual devotion to
religion and family. Justice Scalia describes their marriage as "old-fashioned
Catholic." "We didn't set out to have nine kids," he notes with a twinkle in his
eye, "but we were playing 'Vatican roulette,' as they used to say [because of the

roots in telecomm / cable

ol]."[7] In addition to raising her large brood
volunteer work in hospitals and at church.
2 and took an associate position at the pres-
Day, Reavis, and Pogue, where he was to
displayed the professional and personal
rest of his career. His colleagues found him
debating skills, gregarious, and warm. With
adept at forging consensus but not at the
iews. In fact, he developed a reputation for
nce he had embraced them.
e Cleveland firm, Scalia decided to leave for
sity of Virginia Law School in 1967, and he
Instead, he alternated between government
positions and chools. In 1971 he became general counsel in
the Nixon administration's Office of Telecommunications Policy, where his work
helped to facilitate the expansion of the cable television industry. After one year,
he received a promotion to the chairmanship of the Administrative Conference

of the United States (an independent study group that investigates issues influencing regulatory agencies), and he served there until 1974. At that time, he left to become assistant attorney general in charge of the Office of Legal Counsel in the Department of Justice during the presidency of Gerald Ford. In that post, Scalia addressed issues left over from the Nixon years, such as ownership of the former president's papers and the proper scope of the CIA and FBI. He began to develop an abiding respect, which would later be reflected in his judicial opinions, for the power of the presidency.

In 1977 Scalia left government service for a year's stint as a visiting law professor at Georgetown University and as a "scholar in residence" at the American Enterprise Institute, a conservative think tank in Washington, D.C. There he interacted with colleagues who constituted the right-wing literati, many of them destined to take influential positions in the Reagan administration of the 1980s. Each day they would gather for a brown-bag lunch and discussion of conservative approaches to public policy. Scalia made the next logical step from AEI to a teaching position in 1977 at the University of Chicago Law School, which attracted prominent conservative legal scholars who firmly believed that government should not impinge on a free-market economy. Scalia and his wife bought an old fraternity house near the university to quarter their large and still-growing family. In 1980–81 Scalia took what would be his last position before ascending the bench, a visiting professorship at Stanford Law School in California. During his academic sojourns, he published articles critical of government regulation.

The Reagan administration, which took office in 1981, considered Professor Scalia for the position of solicitor general but opted instead to nominate him to the United States Circuit Court of Appeals for the District of Columbia. His nomination was remarkably uncontested, with his confirmation hearing before the Senate Judiciary Committee covering only two pages in the record book. In August 1982 he was sworn in to his position on the tribunal that has been called second in importance only to the Supreme Court. His colleagues there described his work habits in language similar to that used by his former partners at the Cleveland law firm. He was charming and good-humored to judges of all ideological stripes and was an able discussant in initial conversations over cases. Nevertheless, when he made up his mind, "he [would] plant his flag and go down in flames with it if he need[ed to]," according to former colleague Abner Mikva. Law clerks for more liberal judges on the D.C. Circuit took to calling him "The Ninopath" for his inflexibility.

Over the next four years, Scalia authored close to 100 opinions. One of the first judges to employ a word processor, he was noted for composing most of his own opinions in his now-famous flamboyant style. His conservative jurisprudence, fashioned over a lifetime, revealed itself in a textualist and originalist approach to constitutional interpretation. The former ties him strictly to the words of the document; the latter to what they meant to the society that adopted them at the Founding. Scalia explains: "I do not believe in the living Constitution, this document that morphs from generation to generation. I favor what some might call the dead Constitution, but I prefer to call it the enduring Constitution."[8] On the appeals court he also displayed his devotion to broad interpretation of executive power, his belief in a limited role for the judiciary, and his loyalty to the separation-of-powers principle. In an opinion widely believed to have been authored by Scalia, a three-judge panel invalidated a key enforcement provision of the so-called Gramm-Rudman-Hollings Act, which was Congress's attempt to balance the ballooning federal budget in the mid-1980s by delegating power to carry out budget cuts to the comptroller general. The panel's reasoning was vintage Scalia, arguing that the comptroller general was removable by Congress and therefore a member of the legislative branch. He could not be granted power to enforce the law, a classic *executive* branch function, without violating the separation of powers. The Supreme Court later affirmed the ruling.

In addition, Scalia was also on record in judicial opinions and/or scholarly commentaries as opposing affirmative action in the form of racial preferences, questioning the basis for the Supreme Court's fashioning of a right to sexual privacy (including abortion rights and consensual homosexual acts), and taking a narrower view than some of his colleagues about what constituted protected expression under the First Amendment. (In dissent from a decision by the D.C. Court of Appeals, he excluded sleeping in Lafayette Square as a form of protest from his list of protected speech.) Some observers have noted that Scalia's commentaries, both on and off the bench, were decidedly in sync with the Reagan administration's positions on a host of issues.

Whether Scalia deliberately wrote, especially in extrajudicial commentaries, to attract the attention of Reagan and his minions is unknowable. Nevertheless, a full year before Scalia's appointment to the Supreme Court, an unnamed White House official told the *New Republic* that nominating Scalia to the nation's high court made good "political sense." The official exclaimed, "What a political symbol. Nino would be the first Italian Catholic on the Court. He's got nine kids. He's warm and friendly. Everybody likes him. He's a brilliant conservative. What more could you want."[9] Moreover, at age fifty, Scalia was nine years younger than his nearest competitor, Judge Robert Bork, a colleague on the D.C. Circuit and also on Reagan's list of potential nominees. That meant that barring ill health or the unlikely event of an ideological conversion, Scalia could carry the conservative judicial tenets of the Reagan administration well into the twenty-first century.

The opportunity to promote Scalia came unexpectedly in June 1986 when Chief Justice Warren Burger announced his retirement from the bench. According to Reagan's attorney general, Edwin Meese, the president used three criteria in making his decision to fill the Burger vacancy: intellectual and lawyerly capability, "integrity," and "a commitment to the interpretation of the law rather than making it from the bench."[10] Following this trio of guidelines, the president promoted Associate Justice William H. Rehnquist to the center chair and offered Judge Scalia the ninth seat on the Court at the end of an Oval Office interview with him. Reagan's announcement of his intention to nominate Scalia noted the candidate's "great personal energy, the force of his intellect, and the depth of his understanding of our constitutional jurisprudence [which] uniquely qualify him for elevation to our highest court."[11] When asked at the press conference whether he expected controversy over his nomination in the Senate, Scalia was typically sardonic: "I have no idea. I'm not a politician."[12]

Scalia had no need to worry. While Rehnquist's nomination to chief justice drew all the fire (he would be confirmed by a 68–31 vote after a nasty Senate battle), Scalia found smooth sailing toward his confirmation. His hearings before the Senate Judiciary Committee, to whom he proudly introduced Maureen and their nine offspring, produced accolades for his professional qualifications and the fact that he would become the first Italian American to sit on the Supreme Court. As Scalia puffed on his pipe, Senators engaged in some moderate verbal sparring with him before unanimously agreeing to approve his nomination. The full Senate confirmed Scalia with nary a negative vote.

Undoubtedly, his meritorious résumé, attractive personality, and ethnic representation propelled his case forward. Perhaps the overriding element in Scalia's favor, however, was the fact that the Republicans controlled the Senate in 1986 by a 53–47 margin over the Democrats. Nevertheless, the Democrats had mounted a vociferous, if unfocused and ultimately unsuccessful, campaign against Rehnquist's promotion. The Rehnquist battle might have drawn some of the fire away from Scalia, leaving the Senate too enervated to take up another political crusade against him. In addition, Reagan's popularity provided support for his nominees. Scalia employed an astute and effective strategy at his hearings by avoiding expansive answers to questions on controversial issues. Finally, many Senators viewed him as simply an ideological clone of Rehnquist, whose seat he would take; they therefore believed he would not alter the balance of the Court's votes.

At the White House on September 26, 1986, Scalia took the oath of office required of all federal employees. Then, smiling broadly, he thanked his wife Maureen "without whom I wouldn't be here, or, if I were here, it wouldn't have been as much fun along the way."[13] At the Supreme Court, he swore a second oath, this one required of all judges, administered by the just-installed Chief Justice Rehnquist.

In nearly a quarter century on the Supreme Court, Justice Scalia has generally exhibited faithfulness to the jurisprudence he enunciated and practiced before coming to the high bench. He has expanded his textualist philosophy in constitutional interpretation to judicial reading of statutes. Thus, he preaches that judicial interpretation of laws is confined to the language of the statutes themselves and should not include so-called legislative history, which encompasses congressional committee reports, floor speeches, and the general intent of the legislature in passing the law, as divined by the judiciary. In 1992 Scalia labeled legislative history "the last hope of lost interpretive causes, the St. Jude of the hagiology of statutory construction."[14]

Continuing his broad interpretation of executive power, Scalia was alone in dissent from the Court's 1988 majority opinion in *Morrison v. Olson*, which upheld the creation of the independent counsel or special prosecutor. Scalia argued that assigning prosecutorial powers, an executive branch function, to an individual selected by a special panel of three federal judges and therefore not answerable to the president of the United States, was a patent violation of the separation-of-powers principle. Under that same principle, he was again the author of a solo dissenting opinion the next year in *Mistretta v. United States*. He disagreed with the majority's validation of the United States Sentencing Commission, maintaining that Congress had unconstitutionally delegated legislative power to the Commission, which was granted authority to determine sentencing guidelines to be followed by federal judges. Scalia was vindicated, however, when the Court ruled in 2005's *U.S. v. Booker* that the mandatory element of federal sentencing guidelines violated the Sixth Amendment's jury trial requirement.

Scalia's commitment to separation of powers, and narrow reading of constitutional and statutory texts, led him to dissent in the slew of cases arising from the post-9/11 war on terrorism. In *Hamdi v. Rumsfeld*, decided in 2004, the Court determined that a U.S. citizen being held as an "enemy combatant" might challenge his imprisonment in federal court. Scalia went a step further in siding with the prisoner. Penning a dissent, joined by Justice John Paul Stevens, Scalia argued that the president may not imprison a U.S. citizen as an enemy combatant unless Congress explicitly authorizes him to do so by suspending the writ of habeas corpus. In Rasul v. Bush, however, Scalia's dissent insisted that habeas corpus rights did not extend to "aliens detained by the United States military overseas, outside the borders of the United States and beyond the territorial jurisdictions of all its courts."[15] Thus, non-citizen enemy combatants, held at the U.S. naval base in Guantanamo Bay, Cuba, did not have the right to challenge their incarceration in U.S. courts, as the majority ruled in 2004's Rasul ruling. When President George W. Bush decided to try one of the "Gitmo" prisoners, Salim Hamdan, al-Qaeda leader Osama bin Laden's driver, by a military commission, the Supreme Court heard his appeal and invalidated the commission. Justice Stevens's majority opinion found the commission not expressly authorized by any congressional act and in violation of the Uniform Code of Military Justice as well as the Geneva Conventions. Scalia's dissent cited Congress's 2005 Detainee Treatment Act, which had removed jurisdiction from the federal courts to hear habeas petitions filed by Guantanamo Bay prisoners. Raising the ante in terrorism rulings, Scalia dissented from the Court's 2008 decision in Boumediene v. Bush. This time he predicted that the majority's overturning Congress's scheme of military commissions for trying "Gitmo" prisoners, and giving them access to federal courts, "will almost certainly cause more Americans to be killed."[16]

Keeping the bar high for approaching courts is one of Scalia's hallmarks. Lack of standing to sue (or failure to show harm), is a primary element of judicial self-restraint, whereby the Court can refuse to reach the merits of a case by determining that the plaintiff has failed to demonstrate a concrete individual injury remediable by law. Scalia invokes standing frequently as part of his general philosophy that unelected judges should restrain themselves in deference to the democratically elected branches. On whether courts should act to establish rights that may be lacking explicit expression in the Constitution or statutes, Scalia has an equally restraintist answer. He asserts that the proper way to address modern controversies over abortion, the death penalty, physician-assisted suicide, and gay rights is to call on legislatures to pass laws supported by the majority of the people. Judicial revision of the eighteenth-century intent of the Constitution violates the document itself. In typically pithy fashion, Scalia has urged in public commentary that "having the Constitution mean whatever five out of nine justices think it ought to mean these days is not flexibility but rigidity." He elaborates: "It is not supposed to be our judgment as to what is the socially desirable answer to all of these questions. That's supposed to be the judgment of Congress, and we do our job correctly when we apply what Congress has written as basically and honestly as possible."[17]

Not surprisingly, some of his most scathing and emotive volleys against what he views as judicial imperialism have been fired in abortion cases. His first opportunity to vote on the abortion issue came in the 1988–89 term's highly charged case of *Webster v. Reproductive Health Services*, in which he willingly sided with the narrow majority upholding substantial state restrictions on abortions. His caustic concurring opinion, however, went a step beyond the majority, chastising Justice Sandra Day O'Connor by name for her refusal to overturn *Roe v. Wade* and attacking the rest of the majority for "needlessly . . . prolong[ing] the Court's self-awarded sovereignty over a field where it has little proper business since the answers to most of the cruel questions posed are political and not juridical. . . ."[18]

When the Court accepted *Planned Parenthood of Southeastern Pennsylvania v. Casey* for its 1991–92 term, Scalia understandably thought the case would provide the vehicle for overturning *Roe*. Justice William Brennan, among the majority in *Roe*, had retired in 1990 and was replaced by Bush appointee Justice David Souter, who conservatives hoped would provide another vote to overturn the original 1973 decision establishing a woman's right to abortion on demand in the first three months of pregnancy. Imagine Scalia's anger when Souter formed a plurality with Justices O'Connor and Anthony Kennedy, *reaffirming* the central holding in *Roe* and only slightly mitigating access to abortion in the first trimester. (Justice Stevens and *Roe*'s author Justice Harry Blackmun supported the plurality but would have upheld the precedent in its entirety.) Scalia poured out his exasperation in one of the dissents filed in the case, accusing the majority of engaging in "a new mode of constitutional adjudication that relies not upon text and traditional practice to determine the law, but upon what the Court calls 'reasoned judgment' which turns out to be nothing but philosophical predilection and moral intuition."[19]

In 2007, with Justice O'Connor in retirement, and replaced by reliable conservative Catholic Justice Samuel Alito, Scalia now had a fifth vote to uphold the federal ban on partial-birth abortions in *Gonzales v. Carhart*. Voting with the narrow majority led by Justice Kennedy, he joined Justice Clarence Thomas's concurring opinion, which declared that the Constitution contains no basis for the abortion rights the Court established in *Casey* and *Roe.*

Victory eluded Scalia, however, in a high-profile gay rights case, *Lawrence v. Texas,* from the 2002–03 term. With Kennedy authoring the opinion for a six-person majority, the Court overturned its 1986 *Bowers v. Hardwick* precedent upholding state bans on sodomy. Justice Kennedy's majority opinion in *Lawrence* voided Texas's prohibition on homosexual anal sex, declaring that the law violated "personal dignity and autonomy." He also cited international laws and conventions to indicate that state statutes against gay sexual practices were out of step with European democracies. Such citations wave a red flag in front of the bullish Scalia. His lead dissent for the minority thundered that the Court's ruling would jeopardize all regulation of morals, including laws criminalizing prostitution, fornication, bigamy, adultery, incest, bestiality, and obscenity.

Justice Scalia is equally supportive of state death penalty statutes, arguing that they are constitutional as long as states apply them with due process. Thus, he was in the minority when the Supreme Court invalidated application of the death penalty to the mentally retarded in *Atkins v. Virginia* (2002) and to juvenile defendants who were older than 15 but younger than 18 when they committed their capital crimes in *Roper v. Simmons* (2005). The cumbersome death penalty machine ground to a halt in 2007 as states awaited the Supreme Court's ruling on their use of a three-drug protocol in executions by lethal injection. Two convicts on Kentucky's death row argued that the trio of drugs administered consecutively might cause paralysis of inmates but leave them conscious and unable to indicate severe pain when the final and fatal drug was administered. Scalia's position was crystal clear in oral argument when he told the counsel for one of the capital defendants that the Eighth Amendment's ban on cruel and unusual punishment did not require states to develop the least painful method of executing criminals. The outcome in *Baze v. Rees* was 7–2 to uphold the lethal injection method of execution as not risking substantial pain so great as to constitute an 8th Amendment violation. Later in 2008, Scalia joined Justice Alito's dissent from the narrow majority's ruling to declare unconstitutional Louisiana's death penalty law for child rapists who do not kill their victims. *Kennedy v. Louisiana* ruled that the ultimate penalty of death should be reserved for murder and crimes against the state. Justice Kennedy's majority opinion, evoking "the evolving standards of decency that mark the progress of a maturing society," is antithetical to Scalia's constitutional interpretation that relies on its framers' "original intentions."

Scalia's text-based analysis of the Constitution and statutes has produced numerous opinions decrying the policy of affirmative action to address perceived societal discrimination on the basis of gender and race. In his first term on the Court, he took the Brennan-led majority to task for approving a local transportation agency's promotion of a female employee over a more qualified male colleague. He argued in forceful, sometimes sarcastic terms, that the Court's ruling in *Johnson v. Transportation Agency, Santa Clara County* actually turned Title VII of the Civil Rights Act of 1964 on its head by approving preferential treatment on the basis of gender, which the Act prohibits. In the Court's landmark 1995 ruling in *Adarand v. Peña*, raising the standard that federal set-aside programs for minority contractors must meet under Fourteenth Amendment Equal Protection Clause analysis, Scalia, joined by Justice Clarence Thomas, contributed a concurring opinion that went a step further than Justice O'Connor's majority opinion. Whereas she and her colleagues allowed that a showing of specific racial discrimination (as opposed to general societal bias) could constitute a "compelling state interest" to uphold preferential treatment as a remedy for minority business owners, Scalia argued that under our color-blind Constitution no state interest could ever be so compelling as to permit racial preferences even to atone for past discrimination.

In the 2003 landmark University of Michigan affirmative action cases, Scalia made the most of his opportunity to speak against the use of race and ethnicity in college and law school admissions. During oral argument he mocked UM's contention that racial diversity in higher education is a compelling state interest, "compelling enough to warrant ignoring the Constitution's prohibition of discrimination on the basis of race."[20] His suggested solution to making the Michigan Law School more diverse was to lower its admissions standards. Simply wanting to remain an elite institution did not justify violating the Fourteenth Amendment's requirement that states afford their citizens equal protection of the laws. He reiterated these arguments in his dissent from Justice O'Connor's *Grutter v. Bollinger* majority opinion ratifying the law school's policy of using race and ethnicity as "plus" factors in admissions decisions. He could take some comfort in winning its companion case, *Gratz v. Bollinger*, where he joined the Rehnquist-led majority to invalidate the UM undergraduate college's system of awarding bonus points to underrepresented minorities (African Americans, Hispanics, and Native Americans) in the admissions process.

In the highly publicized 1996 case testing the constitutionality of Virginia Military Institute's all-male admissions policy, Scalia found himself in lonely dissent from Justice Ruth Bader Ginsburg's majority opinion striking down VMI's tradition of excluding women from its state-funded program. He returned once more to his textualist and originalist reading of the Constitution, which he noted did not expressly prohibit the long American tradition of government-funded military schools for men. He compared their existence to the policy of sending exclusively men into combat, a tradition upheld by the Court in the 1981 case sanctioning the male-only draft law. In his *VMI* dissent, and his equally angry opposition to the Court's ruling in the 1996 Colorado gay-rights case, voiding a state constitutional amendment that barred local ordinances banning discrimination on the basis of gender orientation, Scalia pointedly accused the majority of advocating the politically correct causes of the legal elite. He happily wrote the Court's opinion in *Lucas v. South Carolina Coastal Council*, however, which many observers saw as the conservative bloc's effort to return property rights to a more even footing with civil rights and liberties. Not surprisingly, he joined Justice O'Connor's 2005 dissent from the 5–4 ruling in *Kelo v. City of New London, Connecticut*, which ruled that the taking of private property for "economic development" satisfied the Fifth Amendment's "public use" requirement.

Although Justice Scalia's consistent attachment to language and history usually produces conservative results, it can lead to surprisingly liberal outcomes. In the emotionally charged 1989 flag-burning case, *Texas v. Johnson*, for example, he voted with the five-person majority, led by Justice Brennan, to sanction a political protester's burning of the American flag as protected expression under the First Amendment. Scalia typically cites the case to illustrate that "[t]here's no room in [my] judicial philosophy for my personal political or religious beliefs." Recalling when *Johnson* was handed down, Scalia has said, "I came down to breakfast the next morning and my wife is humming 'Stars and Stripes Forever.' This does not make for a happy camper."[21]

His understanding of Fourth Amendment standards regarding unreasonable searches and seizure propelled him to vote with another liberal majority, and even write its opinion, refusing to extend the "plain view" exception to a warrantless search that had discovered stolen stereo equipment. The facts in *Arizona v. Hicks* (1987) indicated that a police officer had moved stereo components to reveal their serial numbers, and to Scalia and his colleagues in the majority the traditional doctrine of "plain view" did not obtain if the suspicious object had been moved, even just a few inches, to reveal its incriminating evidence. He also wrote for the majority in *Kyllo v. U.S.* (2001) to invalidate federal agents' use of a thermal-imaging device aimed at a private home from a public street to detect heat emanating from the house. Law enforcement agents used the devices to determine if residents were growing marijuana plants under special lighting. Scalia determined that the tactic constituted a "search" within the meaning of the Fourth Amendment and was unreasonable without a warrant.

In another Fourth Amendment case (*National Treasury Employees Union v. Von Raab* [1989]), Scalia dissented from the Court's ruling upholding mandatory drug testing for customs employees, finding it an unreasonable search and seizure. In 1995's *Vernonia School District v. Acton*, however, his majority opinion sanctioned random drug-testing by urinalysis for student athletes, citing the reasonableness of the policy and the low expectation of privacy on the part of athletes. Seven years later, in *Board of Education of Independent School District No. 92 of Pottawatomie City v. Earls*, he voted with the Court to extend the *Vernonia* precedent to an Oklahoma school district's random drug-testing policy for all middle- and high-school students participating in any extracurricular activities.

Undoubtedly, Justice Scalia would have preferred to find a constitutional formula to limit flag-burning, uphold convictions of a stereo thief and marijuana-grower, and discourage drug use among customs officials, but he could not. As he noted in a 1989 law review article, the rule of law is a law of rules, which must be applied neutrally by the judge regardless of his personal preferences.

His interpretation of the religion clauses of the First Amendment, however, often returns him to the conservative fold. Scalia upheld for a 7-2 Court Ohio's policy of allowing the Ku Klux Klan to erect a cross in front of the state's capitol building, although his opinion focused on the free-speech right of the KKK to expression in a classic public forum (*Capitol Square Review Board v. Pinette* [1995]). He was livid in dissent from Justice Kennedy's 5-4 *Lee v. Weisman* (1992) opinion voiding invocations and benedictions at public school graduations. Scalia accused the majority of engaging in "social engineering" and basing its ruling on "the changeable philosophical predilections of the justices of this Court." The latter charge was a not-so-veiled reference to the fact that Kennedy had changed his vote in the case between the Court's conference and its drafting of opinions, thus transforming Scalia's vote from a majority to minority position. Equally galling to him was Justice Souter's 1994 majority opinion in *Board of Education of Kiryas Joel Village v. Grument*, which struck down New York's creation of a separate school district for a community of Hasidic Jews. Scalia repeatedly argued that the Founding Fathers had created a constitutional tradition of religious toleration that the Court had violated with its extreme separationist rulings.

Nevertheless, religious toleration has its limits, as demonstrated by Scalia's ruling in the 1990 *Employment Division, Department of Human Resources of Oregon v. Smith* case, in which Native Americans challenged the state's prohibition of peyote use. Because the hallucinogenic drug is a staple of Indian liturgy, the plaintiffs argued that the Oregon law violated their free-exercise-of-religion rights under the First Amendment. Scalia wrote for the six-person majority that the Oregon law could be sustained because it was not directly aimed at religious practices. Its general applicability had only an "incidental" impact on religion.

The Oregon case also demonstrates Scalia's support of legislative pronouncements unless they impinge on constitutional principles as he perceives them. Federalism, with a general emphasis on state power, receives high priority in his jurisprudence. Thus, he wrote the Court's 1997 opinion striking down the unfunded mandates imposed on the states by the Brady Gun-Control Law (*Printz v. U.S.*) and voted with the 1995 majority that invalidated the Gun-Free School Zones Act as reaching beyond the Congress's commerce power and impinging on state prerogatives (*U.S. v. Lopez*). Not surprisingly, Scalia voted, in dissent, to uphold the right of twenty-two states to establish term limits for their members of Congress (*U.S. Term Limits, Inc. v. Thornton* [1995]).

Yet in one of the Court's most controversial decisions in its long history, *Bush v. Gore*, Scalia sided with the majority against the Florida Supreme Court's decision to continue a recount of votes in the 2000 presidential election. He joined the *per curiam* ruling that the standardless recounting procedures ran afoul of equal protection guarantees, as well as Chief Justice Rehnquist's concurrence, which added due process violations to the Florida Supreme Court's list of errors. In media interviews nearly a decade later, he impatiently admonishes critics of the ruling, ranging from the Oxford University debating society to *The Daily Show* host Jon Stewart, "Get over it!" George W. Bush would have won even without the Court's intervention, according to unofficial recounts of the Florida ballots, Scalia argues. Defensively, he delineates other reasons that criticism of the Court is unfounded: Bush was reelected in 2004; the Court had nothing to do with his decision to invade Iraq after 9/11; Vice President Al Gore brought the litigation to the courts, and the U.S. Supreme Court had to uphold the federal Constitution against a state court's rulings.

Scalia's originalism/textualism produced headlines again at the end of the Supreme Court's 2007–08 term. Writing for a minimal majority of five in *Heller*, he determined that Washington, D.C.'s ban on handgun ownership violated the Second Amendment's "right of the people to keep and bear arms."

His overall voting profile on the Court certainly places him squarely in the conservative camp. Scalia found an ideological soulmate when Justice Thomas joined the high bench in 1991. During a typical term, they are in agreement over 80 percent of the time. The most common alignment in closely divided cases is Roberts, Scalia, Kennedy, Thomas, and Alito. The above litany of majority opinions indicates that Scalia can write for colleagues and command a majority. Nevertheless, he also has earned a reputation for solo dissents, often written in a patented acerbic, occasionally mean-spirited, style. Some observers initially questioned his breadth of influence if the latter pattern were to continue, but Judge Alex Kozinski of the Ninth Circuit Court of Appeals maintains that the sheer number and weight of Scalia's ideas will ensure his influence over the length of his extended tenure on the Court. Nevertheless, his reputation for singling out colleagues for criticism in his pointed dissents, and his advancing age, probably combined to deny him the chief justice's chair when Rehnquist died in 2005. Bush selected the congenial John Roberts, nearly two decades Scalia's junior. Now past seventy, he admits to considering retirement when he turned sixty-five, but he questioned what could he do as an encore. Nothing is as "interesting and satisfying" as serving on the highest court in the land. He jokes that he is, in effect, "working for free" because federal judges retire at full pay.[22] Now the grandfather of twenty-eight, Scalia is obviously proud of his offsprings' accomplishments. He teases that son Paul "took one for the team" by entering the priesthood, making up for two of his brothers who followed in their father's footsteps and became lawyers. The justice speaks glowingly of another son who graduated from West Point and has risen to the rank of major.

In the midst of the 2007–08 term, Scalia took to the airwaves to tout his co-authored book, *Making Your Case*, a guide to oral advocacy. After years of refusing to appear on television, and engaging in dust-ups with journalists who tried to record his public lectures, he decided to "come out of the closet." At the urging of friends and family, Scalia began to do televised interviews on CBS, PBS, and C-SPAN. If he is going to be a public figure, he noted, gleefully citing the fact that he is the most popular "bobble-head" justice sold on the Internet, he thought Americans should hear from him first hand. When shown a clip of Jon Stewart mocking him on *The Daily Show*, Scalia smiled and replied, "Once was enough [to watch the program]." He found the comedian's schtick "childish" and noted that "you can be humorous *and* accurate at the same time."[23]

While "The Ninopath" can slice an opposing justice's opinion to ribbons, he maintains a playful side that allowed him to appear on stage as an opera extra in eighteenth-century costume (including powdered wig and knee breeches) with friend and colleague Justice Ruth Bader Ginsburg. Despite their judicial differences, she enjoys their friendship because, she says quite simply, he makes her laugh. He has also been spotted leading sing-alongs at Court receptions, where he belts out "oldies" to piano accompaniment with gusto. But he cannot be dismissed as a ham or judicial comedian; his philosophy, intellect, and personality will remain forces to be contended with for as long as he sits on the Supreme Court (in whatever he wishes to call his seat!).

Recently, Justice Scalia sat in an artist's studio, posing for an oil portrait, commissioned by his former law clerks. According to tradition, the painting will one day hang at the Court after he retires or passes on. The props he chose to surround himself with in the portrait illustrate the most meaningful aspects of his professional, personal, and spiritual lives: a copy of *The Federalist* (Madison's, Hamilton's, and Jay's interpretation of the Constitution); *Webster's Second International Dictionary* (not the newer third edition, which he finds inferior); a wedding photo of Maureen; and a portrait of Thomas More, Antonin Scalia's saintly hero, whom Henry VIII martyred for following the doctrines of the Roman Catholic Church. Never have artistic symbols so accurately summarized a justice's life.

CHAPTER FOUR

Anthony M. Kennedy

Anthony Kennedy has a genuine dramatic flair. He once participated in a moot court based on the *dramatis personae* of a Shakespearean play, took roles in Washington, D.C., productions of Ibsen's *Peer Gynt* and Strauss's *Die Fledermaus* (along with his colleagues Justices Ruth Bader Ginsburg and Stephen Breyer), and delivered lectures dressed as James Madison. Beyond the realm of playacting, however, he also knows when a dramatic turn of phrase can capture the profundity of his work as a Supreme Court justice. Prior to announcing his crucial vote in the closely decided 1992 Pennsylvania abortion case *Planned Parenthood of Southeastern Pennsylvania v. Casey,* he excused himself from a reporter, saying, "I need to brood. . . . It's a moment of quiet around here to search your soul and your conscience."[1] He is also an eloquent advocate of the Court he serves and the rule of law in American society. In his earnest temperament, inspiring eloquence, and bespectacled visage, he is the very model of the judge/lawyer/professor he plays in real life.

Life began for Anthony McLeod Kennedy on July 23, 1936, in Sacramento, California, the home of his father, Anthony J. ("Bud") Kennedy, and his mother, Gladys ("Sis") McLeod Kennedy. Bud Kennedy was a successful lawyer and lobbyist at the California state legislature. His wife Sis, a 1928 graduate of Stanford University, worked as a teacher and then a secretary in the California Senate, where she met her future husband, whom she married in 1932. The Kennedys had three children (two boys and a girl); Anthony was the middle child. Their home in Sacramento, a white, two-story colonial built by Mr. Kennedy, was a hub of political, civic, and social activity. Among the elder Kennedy's associates were California Governor Earl Warren, the future chief justice of the United States, and other prominent politicians.

Thus, from his early childhood young Anthony Kennedy circulated among California's most celebrated citizens. While still in grade school, he began serving as a page in the California Senate, a position arranged by his parents. When his father was trying cases, he would sometimes invite his son to accompany him to court. The future justice estimated that he had witnessed ten jury trials before he was even out of high school.

At McClatchy High School in Sacramento, Anthony routinely made the honor roll and won awards from the California Scholarship Federation. He experienced a remarkably trouble-free boyhood that included regular service as an altar boy at his Roman Catholic parish church. One of his friends described Kennedy's reputation: "When we were growing up, if any of us were going to do something naughty, Tony would go home."[2] Kennedy used to joke with his friends that his father, in a fit of affectionate despair, had offered to pay him $100 if just once he would do something requiring his parents to come pick him up at the local police station! The youngster never collected on the dare.

Kennedy always assumed that he would attend Stanford, as had his mother, and become a lawyer, as did his father. Kennedy indeed followed in his parents' footsteps. As an undergraduate majoring in history and political science, the future justice continued his outstanding academic career at Stanford. He was particularly captivated by constitutional law, and his professor for that class described him as brilliant. Kennedy completed his graduation requirements in three years, but his father apparently thought his son was too young to enroll immediately in law school, so young Tony spent a year at the London School of Economics. Upon his return in 1958, he received his B.A. degree from Stanford, where he was elected to Phi Beta Kappa. He then attended Harvard Law School, from which he obtained his degree, *cum laude*, in 1961. Competing against the many superstars at the institution, he did not make law review.

After a six-month stint in the California Army National Guard, he began his practice of law in the prestigious San Francisco firm of Thelen, Marrin, John & Bridges, but within two years he was back in Sacramento to assume the law practice of his father, who had died suddenly of a heart attack in 1963. For four years he worked in the solo practice and then became a partner in the firm of Evans, Jackson, and Kennedy, where he remained until 1975. He assumed his father's lobbying duties, but, described as an intellectual, Kennedy seemingly disliked the flesh-pressing and glad-handing required of such work in the state capitol. Eventually, he found an outlet for his more academic interest in the law when the dean of McGeorge School of Law at the University of the Pacific offered him a part-time teaching position. Just as in his student days, he thrived in the classroom and would often amaze his students by lecturing for three hours on constitutional law without referring to a note.

In 1963 Kennedy had married Mary Jeanne Davis, a Stanford graduate and elementary school teacher, and they eventually had three children, Justin, Gregory, and Kristin, all of whom are Stanford graduates. The Kennedys raised the children in the Sacramento home built by their paternal grandfather, where Anthony had spent his own happy childhood.

Like Bud Kennedy, the future justice was a Republican, if not a particularly active one. Nevertheless, in the early 1970s he was asked to serve on a commission to draft a tax-limitation initiative known as Proposition 1 for California Governor Ronald Reagan. Although the ballot proposition failed in 1973, a similar proposal passed in 1978, fomenting a taxpayer revolution in the Golden State. Moreover, Kennedy had impressed the Reagan camp with the constitutional expertise he brought to the commission. When an opening became available on the U.S. Court of Appeals for the Ninth Circuit in 1975, Reagan recommended Kennedy to President Gerald Ford, who appointed the thirty-eight-year-old Californian to the bench, making him the youngest federal appellate judge in the country.

Kennedy would spend the next thirteen years on the Ninth Circuit, watching it expand from thirteen active judges when he joined it in 1975 to twenty-three jurists during the presidential administration of Jimmy Carter from 1977 to 1981. Carter filled the expanded circuit with his appointments, rendering it the most liberal in the nation. In this ideological context, Judge Kennedy was known as a conservative, but one more in touch with the Gerald Ford than the Barry Goldwater wing of the Republican Party. As a jurist, Kennedy was thorough, respectful of precedent, and open-minded. He simply refused to confine himself in any jurisprudential straitjacket.

Of the 430 opinions that Judge Kennedy wrote on the Ninth Circuit, one of the most important was in *Immigration and Naturalization Service v. Chadha*, a 1980 case in which he ruled that the "legislative veto," allowing one or both houses of Congress to block executive branch decisions, was an unconstitutional violation of the separation of powers. The U.S. Supreme Court affirmed his decision in 1983. Another 1980 Kennedy opinion attracted more headlines at the time he wrote it. In *Beller v. Middendorf* he asserted that U.S. Navy regulations prohibiting homosexual conduct were constitutional. He did not dismiss the possibility that the Constitution might afford a right to sexual privacy in civilian contexts. Five years later Kennedy angered women's rights groups by overturning a ruling that would have mandated that the state of Washington compensate female employees millions of dollars for their "comparable worth" to men in similar jobs. In

AFSCME v. State of Washington, Judge Kennedy argued for the Ninth Circuit that the discrepancy between pay for men and women in Washington was *not* the demonstrable result of gender-based discrimination.

Judge Kennedy was marking a dozen years on the federal appellate bench when Justice Lewis F. Powell, Jr., unexpectedly announced his retirement from the U.S. Supreme Court in June 1987. No commentator failed to report the ramifications for the tribunal's future direction. Indeed, Powell had played a pivotal role as the tie-breaking vote in cases determining the Court's interpretation of constitutional law on abortion, affirmative action, and separation of church and state. He was neither consistently liberal nor conservative but had swayed the Court's decisional outcomes from one ideological camp to another by virtue of his "swing vote."

President Ronald Reagan and his advisors badly misjudged the impact of "swing seat" politics on the appointment process when they nominated Judge Robert Bork of the U.S. Circuit Court of Appeals for the District of Columbia to fill Powell's position. Unquestionably qualified by virtue of his intellect, education, and experience, he was, nevertheless, stridently conservative in his long "paper trail" of judicial opinions and scholarship. With the Democrats in control of the Senate, the Bork hearings before the Judiciary Committee were a bloodbath. Bork's commitment to a jurisprudence of original intent of the Founding Fathers appeared rigid and was fair game for being portrayed as beyond the mainstream of contemporary judicial philosophy. Moreover, Bork's personal appearance and demeanor seemed as suspect as his ideology. His devilish beard and sometimes turgid academic discourse did not endear him to senators, liberal interest groups, or the public. Nor did his detailed, lecture-like answers to every conceivable question posed to him by the Senate Judiciary Committee. No careful observer of the drama over filling the "swing seat" could have been surprised by the ultimate denouement that saw Bork's nomination go down in a resounding 42–58 defeat in the Senate.

Reagan's vindictive nomination of Judge Douglas Ginsburg, also of the D.C. Circuit Court of Appeals, rubbed salt in the appointment battle wounds. Ginsburg was a young devotee of the conservative "Law and Economics Movement." Although he lacked the paper trail of his predecessor Bork, a long fight over his nomination loomed in the Senate. Only the startling disclosure of his past marijuana use, both as a student and as a law professor, saved the country from another wrangle over the nomination of a perceived extremist for Powell's crucial seat.

In his third attempt to fill the vacant spot on the nation's high court, President Reagan turned to Anthony Kennedy, announcing his nomination on November 11, 1987—five months after Justice Powell had made public his departure from the bench. In selecting Kennedy, Reagan described him as a popular judge who had established a record on the Ninth Circuit that was fair but tough in applying the law. The president also labeled Kennedy "a true conservative . . . who believes that our constitutional system is one of enumerated powers."[3] After the Bork and Ginsburg disasters, Reagan's minions must have been drawn to Judge Kennedy's profile in the 1987 *Almanac of the Federal Judiciary*, describing him as "courteous, stern on the bench, somewhat conservative, bright, well-prepared, filled with nervous energy, asks many questions, good analytical mind, not afraid to break new ground, open-minded, good business lawyer, hard to peg, an enigma, tends to agonize over opinions."[4]

By virtue of his moderately conservative judicial record, his moral propriety, and his pleasant appearance and personality, Kennedy appeared to be the antithesis of Robert Bork or Douglas Ginsburg. There was no doubt that Kennedy's decisions during his long tenure on the appellate bench produced conservative results, but his opinions seemed more narrowly crafted than Bork's. Thus Kennedy could plausibly argue in his written responses to a standard Judiciary Committee questionnaire that "[l]ife tenure is a constitutional mandate to the federal judiciary to proceed with caution, to avoid reaching issues not necessary to the resolution of the suit at hand, and to defer to the political process."[5] On the issue of judicial philosophy, he added, "It's somewhat difficult for me to offer myself as someone with a complete cosmology of the Constitution. I do not have an overarching theory, a unitary theory of interpretation. . . . I think if a judge decides a case because he or she is committed to a result, that it destroys confidence in the legal system."[6]

On December 14, 1987, the opening day of the Kennedy hearings, the Supreme Court split 4–4 on a case involving the constitutionality of an Illinois law requiring minors wanting abortions to notify their parents. The tie vote only heightened the urgency of filling Justice Powell's seat on the Court that had been vacant since June. Anthony Kennedy's record and performance at his confirmation hearings convinced the Senate Judiciary Committee that he was the perfect choice to fill the vacancy. The committee report, which unanimously endorsed Kennedy's nomination, described him as "open-minded, fair, and independent," and as possessing "the truly judicious qualities that Justice Lewis Powell embodied."[7] Accepting the committee's unqualified approval, the full Senate voted on

February 3, 1998 to confirm Kennedy's nomination 97-0. He took two oaths of office, one at the White House and one at the Court, on February 18, 1988, and started work immediately on the Court's term that was already half over. Fortunately, his thirteen years as a federal judge on an appellate court prepared him for the rigors of work at the Supreme Court, so there was no "freshman effect" causing him to maintain a low profile.

By 1989 Kennedy's voting record and several majority opinions already distinguished him from Justice Powell. Instead of functioning as a vote that balanced the liberal and conservative blocs by siding with one or the other from case to case (as had Justice Powell), Kennedy's vote began to tip the balance most often in favor of the conservatives. In the abortion realm, for example, Kennedy voted with the 5-4 majority in *Webster v. Reproductive Health Services* to allow states the right to impose substantial new restrictions on abortion. Kennedy also arrived at a conservative result on the matter of the right to privacy and the drug-testing issue. In *Skinner v. Railway Labor Executives* and *National Treasury Employees v. Von Raab*, he wrote both majority opinions for the Court's constitutional sanction of the federal government's efforts to create a drug-free workplace.

In the area of affirmative action, Justice Kennedy began to distance himself most fundamentally from Justice Powell. In early 1989 Kennedy voted with the 6-3 majority in *City of Richmond v. J.A. Croson Co.*, invalidating a local set-aside law in Richmond, Virginia, that channeled 30 percent of public works funds to minority-owned construction companies. He also cast his vote with the narrow 5-4 majorities that reached conservative results in two additional 1989 affirmative action/employment discrimination cases in *Martin v. Wilks* and *Wards Cove Packing v. Atonio*.

In just his first full term on the high court, Kennedy's most notable contribution to the tribunal's more conservative tack in employment discrimination cases was his 1989 majority opinion in *Patterson v. McLean Credit Union*, which upheld the use of the 1866 Civil Rights Act for claims of discrimination at the initial hiring stage but barred use of the statute for claims of on-the-job bias.

In church-state matters Kennedy revealed a conservative accommodationist stance, particularly in simultaneous 1989 rulings in *Allegheny County v. Greater Pittsburgh A.C.L.U.* on Christmas season displays, sponsored by city and county governments in Pittsburgh. He dissented from a decision declaring that a Nativity scene, unaccompanied by any more secular symbols of the season, amounted to an unconstitutional endorsement of the Christian faith. He found himself in the majority, however, when the Court permitted a Hanukkah menorah to be displayed next to a Christmas tree.

Another 1989 First Amendment case, this time in the free expression realm, found Kennedy uncharacteristically joining a liberal decision in *Texas v. Johnson*, which declared via Justice William Brennan's opinion that burning the American flag as a political protest is a form of protected symbolic speech. Kennedy was uncomfortable enough with his vote in the majority that he penned a concurring opinion to explain that "[t]he hard fact is that sometimes we must make decisions we do not like. We make them because they are right, right in the sense that the law and the Constitution, as we see them, compel the result."[8] Kennedy's vote and rationale for it signaled that in some instances he might behave more like the justice he replaced, Lewis Powell, judging each decision on a case-by-case basis.

The voting line-ups on the Supreme Court in the 1990s bear witness to that assessment of Kennedy's role. In church-state cases, he perplexed conservatives with his 1992 majority opinion in *Lee v. Weisman*, arguing that nonsectarian prayers at public school graduation ceremonies violated the First Amendment's Establishment Clause because they were coercive. Justice Antonin Scalia's dissent for four members of the Court labeled the decision "senseless" and "unsupported in law."[9] Kennedy also joined the majority two years later in *Board of Education of Kiryas Joel Village v. Grumet*, which invalidated New York's creation of a separate school district for a community of Satmar Hasidic Jews so that their handicapped and special education children would not have to attend public schools. In the 1995 case of *Rosenberger v. University of Virginia*, however, he argued for the narrow five-person majority that Rosenberger's free expression rights to publish a student-run Christian magazine trumped the University's argument that to provide him with funds raised from student activities fees would violate the Establishment Clause.

In cases involving the free exercise of religion, Kennedy joined the majority in the 1990 landmark decision of *Employment Division, Department of Human Resources of Oregon v. Smith*, upholding the state's prohibition on liturgical use of peyote (a hallucinogenic drug) by Native Americans. Justice Scalia's opinion held that the First Amendment's Free Exercise Clause did not ban "generally applicable" laws that have only an "incidental" effect on religious practices. In response to the decision, Congress passed the Religious Freedom Restoration Act of 1993 that required laws to meet a higher standard, known as a "compelling state interest," if they impinged on religious practices. Justice Kennedy, applying the reasoning from *Smith*, produced the Court's opinion in its unanimous 1993 decision, *Church of the Lukumi Babalu Aye v. Hialeah*, striking down the Florida city's ban on animal sacrifices, which all nine justices viewed as a direct attack on the Cuban American Santeria sect's religious practice of killing animals. Nevertheless, in 1997 Kennedy penned the opinion for a 6–3 Court invalidating the Religious Freedom Restoration Act in *City of Boerne v. Flores*. He and his colleagues in the majority viewed the act as a congressional usurpation of the Court's power to determine the parameters of constitutional protection of religion and an intrusion on the states' authority to make laws.

Kennedy's fealty to the separation of powers (dividing the roles of the three branches of government according to constitutional mandates) and federalism (assigning powers to national and state levels of government again by constitutional directives), was evident in *Flores*. His loyalty to the twin principles of American constitutionalism had also been present in his 1995 deciding vote in *United States v. Lopez*, invalidating a federal law, which banned guns near schools, and restricting Congress's commerce power. Yet in that same term he sided with the interests of the national government, rather than the states, when he cast another deciding vote, this time in *U.S. Term Limits v. Thornton*, striking down state laws limiting the terms of their members of Congress. His concurring opinion emphasized the "distinctive character" of the federal government and added, "There can be no doubt, if we are to respect the republican origins of the Nation and preserve its federal character, that there exists a federal right of citizenship, a relationship between the people of the Nation and their National Government, with which the states may not interfere."[10] On two additional federalism cases, involving the national attempt to regulate drugs, Kennedy split between the federal government and the states based on the facts in the cases and his careful reading of applicable statutes. He voted with the majority in *Gonzales v. Raich* (2005) to uphold the federal government's authority, under the Controlled Substances Act, passed by Congress as part of its interstate commerce power, to regulate locally grown marijuana in California, which allowed its use for medicinal purposes. One year later, however, Kennedy wrote the majority opinion in *Gonzales v. Oregon* striking down the U.S. attorney general's attempts to regulate doctors' distribution of controlled substances, under the same act, for use in physician-assisted suicides of competent terminally ill individuals, a legal procedure under Oregon law. Kennedy argued that the federal Controlled Substances Act was silent on practice of medicine and left to state regulation the actions of physicians.

In *Bush v. Gore*, stopping the Florida recount of disputed votes in the 2000 presidential election, Justice Kennedy gave priority to his sense of the national government's primacy and the Supreme Court's supremacy. He joined the Court's *per curiam* opinion and, indeed, may have been its author, for it reflects his reasoning in *Boerne* regarding the role of the nation's highest tribunal to settle constitutional disputes. As he told a congressional committee a few months after the historic election ruling that effectively made George W. Bush president, "It involved a constitutional issue of the gravest importance, decided 4 to 3 by a *state* court on a *federal* issue, . . . it was our responsibility to take the case."[11] In addition, the justices' *per curiam* holding reflects Kennedy's reasoning on *individual* equality (not a *group-based* conception of the principle commonly embraced by more liberal jurists interpreting the Fourteenth Amendment), which he and all but two of his colleagues (John Paul Stevens and Ruth Bader Ginsburg) believed the standardless Florida recounting procedures violated. In *Rice v. Cayetano*, decided the previous term on Fifteenth Amendment grounds, Kennedy had penned the majority opinion invalidating Hawaii's limitation of voting for the Office of Hawaiian Affairs to "native" Hawaiians. For Kennedy, and the same six justices (Rehnquist, O'Connor, Scalia, Thomas, Souter, Breyer) who would vote to stop Florida's chaotic ballot recount a few months later, Hawaii's voting regulations did not honor the equality of each individual citizen.

Justice Kennedy's record in race decisions reflects a consistently conservative pattern. He wrote for a unanimous Court in the 1992 case of *Freeman v. Pitts* that racially segregated schools resulting from private choice, not state action, are not subject to constitutional remedies. That same year, in a voting case from Alabama, he held for the majority in *Presley v. Etowah County Commission* that two counties were not required under the Voting Rights Act of 1965 to abolish their new system of road management that had reduced the effective power of newly elected black commissioners. Kennedy's opinion two years later in *Holder v. Hall* ruled for a 5–4 Court that the size of a governmental body cannot be challenged under the Voting Rights Act as diluting the influence of minority voters because no legal standard exists for determining the "fair" number of representatives. He followed that decision with the 1995 redistricting ruling in which he concluded for another 5–4 majority that race could not be the "predominant factor" used in drawing majority-minority districts (*Miller v. Johnson*).

Justice Kennedy could also be found with the narrow majority holding in 1995's *Adarand v. Peña* that federal set-aside programs favoring minority contractors must be held to the highest compelling state interest standard. In the 2003

University of Michigan affirmative action cases, Kennedy voted to strike down the policies at both the UM Law School and undergraduate college, which placed him in dissent on the former and in the majority on the latter. In dissenting from Justice Sandra Day O'Connor's ruling to uphold the law school's use of race as a "plus" in admissions to create a diverse student body, Kennedy argued that the Court's majority had failed to examine the policy with the required "strict scrutiny."

Justice Kennedy has also remained consistent in his conservative analysis of most criminal rights, which he developed on the lower appellate court. Yet he has notably switched positions on several aspects of the death penalty. In his first complete term on the high tribunal in 1989, he sided with Justice Scalia and three other justices to uphold capital punishment for juveniles in *Stanford v. Kentucky*. By 2005, however, his view had shifted. In *Roper v. Simmons*, Kennedy provided the fifth vote to strike down death penalties applied to defendants older than 15 but younger than 18 when they committed their capital crimes. He noted that over three-quarters of the states that apply capital punishment no longer do so for juvenile offenders. In addition, international opinion had turned against the juvenile death penalty. Three years earlier, Kennedy had joined the six-justice majority to invalidate the application of death sentences to the mentally retarded in *Atkins v. Virginia*. Justice Stevens assigned Kennedy the opinion of the Court in 2008's *Kennedy v. Louisiana*, in which the tribunal ruled that capital punishment must apply only to murder and crimes against the state, not to child rape. On the issue of whether current lethal injection procedures violated the Eighth Amendment's ban on cruel and unusual punishment, however, Kennedy voted with the 7–2 majority to rule that they did not (*Baze v. Rees*).

In matters of privacy and gender, he has raised conservatives' ire for reaching liberal results. The abortion issue produced voting blocs along three different fault lines in the 1992 *Casey* decision. There were four votes to overturn *Roe v. Wade*: Chief Justice Rehnquist and Justice Byron White (the two dissenters in *Roe* when the case was handed down in 1973), and Justices Scalia and Thomas. Two justices in the five-person majority wished to uphold *Roe* in its entirety: Justice Harry Blackmun (*Roe*'s author) and Justice Stevens. Justices Kennedy, Souter, and O'Connor formed a three-person plurality whose opinion upheld the "central holding" of *Roe* while abolishing its cumbersome trimester system for determining when women have the right to terminate their pregnancies. In its place they substituted the "undue burden" test, which allowed state restrictions on abortion even in the first trimester as long as they did not pose "substantial" obstacles to a woman seeking such a procedure. The trio's stunning opinion emphasized the Court's need to uphold precedent as a means of protecting its legitimacy; overturning the two-decades-old decision, around which many in society had ordered their lives, would irreparably damage the Court's authority, according to the plurality's reasoning.

When the matter of so-called partial-birth abortions came before the justices, however, Kennedy landed firmly in the conservative camp. In 2000, that position placed him in dissent when Justice Stephen Breyer ruled for the 5-4 Court that Nebraska's ban on such procedures posed an "undue burden" on women and provided no exception to preserve the health of the mother (*Stenberg v. Carhart*). Seven years later, Justice Kennedy's opinion became law in *Gonzales v. Carhart*, which upheld the federal prohibition of partial-birth abortions. The replacement of Justice O'Connor, who had voted with the majority in *Stenberg*, by conservative Justice Samuel Alito meant five votes now existed to ban such abortion procedures nationwide.

Romer v. Evans, decided by the Court in 1996, was a closely watched case that touched on the contentious issue of gay rights. After several cities in Colorado passed ordinances banning discrimination based on sexual orientation, Colorado voters adopted an amendment to the state's constitution precluding such protection of homosexuals or bisexuals. Led by Justice Kennedy's opinion, a 6-3 Court invalidated the Colorado amendment on the grounds that it violated the federal Fourteenth Amendment's Equal Protection Clause by disqualifying one class of persons from seeking governmental safeguards. Even under the lowest level of Equal Protection analysis (the "rational relation" test), the state amendment was fatally flawed in both its application and justification. It singled out one class of persons, denied them the prospect of legal protection, and seemed motivated by animosity toward the class rather than a legitimate governmental purpose.

Justice Kennedy also relied on the Fourteenth Amendment, this time the liberty component of its Due Process Clause, to void Texas's law against homosexual sodomy for a 6-3 Court in the 2003 *Lawrence* case. He argued in the landmark ruling that Texas's law supported no legitimate state interest that would allow such "intrusion into the personal and private life of the individual."[12] His decisions to strike down the juvenile death penalty and anti-sodomy laws placed him on conservative interest groups' hit lists; some even called for his impeachment.

On the last day of the Court's 1997-98 Term, Justice Kennedy announced the majority opinion in *Burlington Industries, Inc. v. Ellerth*. By the same vote (7-2), and with the same justices in dissent (Thomas and Scalia), the Court ruled in this case and *Faragher v. City of Boca Raton* that an employer is vicariously liable for actionable sexual harassment perpetrated by a superior, subject to an affirmative defense by the employer that considers the reasonableness of his conduct and that of the victim. Kennedy and Souter, who wrote in *Faragher*, expanded legal recourse for victims of sexual harassment, thus filling a gap in federal statutory law left unaddressed by Congress. Yet Kennedy joined the five-justice majority to rule that a woman who claimed nearly two decades of pay discrimination by her employer had waived her right to sue the company under Title VII of the 1964 Civil Rights Act because she did not file within 180 days of the initial discriminatory act (*Ledbetter v. Goodyear Tire* [2007]).

Justice Kennedy, like Justice Powell before him, has often provided the pivotal swing vote in closely decided cases, particularly after Justice O'Connor's retirement in 2006. In the first full term (2006–07) with President George W. Bush's two appointees, Chief Justice John Roberts and Justice Samuel Alito, in place, Kennedy played the role of pivotal justice. Of that term's 68 total cases, about one-third (24), a particularly large proportion, were decided by 5–4 margins. Justice Kennedy voted with the majority in all of those closely divided cases, and he dissented only twice the entire term. Nineteen of the 5–4 decisions in 2006–07 split along identifiable ideological lines, with 13 (54 percent) reaching a conservative result, led by Kennedy, Scalia, Thomas, Roberts, and Alito. Among Kennedy's crucial votes in high-profile cases that term was the previously mentioned ruling upholding the ban on partial-birth abortions, along with the invalidation of public schools' voluntary use of race and ethnicity in school assignments to promote diversity (*Parents Involved in Community Schools v. Seattle School District No. 1* and *Meredith v. Jefferson County [Ky.] Board of Education*). Kennedy wrote a separate concurrence, however, to distinguish his reasoning from the more conservative majority. As in the 2003 Michigan affirmative action cases, he accepted diversity in education as a legitimate state interest, but he thought that Seattle's and Jefferson County's use of race and ethnicity to assign children to schools was impermissible. School districts could, he argued, consider the racial make-up of neighborhoods when determining the sites for future schools and could take into consideration the race of students who might be attracted to certain academic programs. Kennedy cast his vote with a liberal outcome in the term's closely watched environmental case, *Massachusetts v. Environmental Protection Agency*. The five-justice majority, led by Stevens, first ruled that Massachusetts had standing to bring suit against the EPA for failure to enforce limits on automobile emissions. Although the federal agency argued that it had no authority to issue such regulations, the Court countered that it did, unless it could prove a scientific reason for refusing to crack down on cars' contribution to the so-call greenhouse effect.

The 2007–08 term produced far fewer 5–4 decisions (only 11 out of 67), and Justice Kennedy's vote did not have the overall impact that it did the previous term. In fact, he dissented in 4 of the closely divided decisions and 10 times total. Yet his votes and opinions carried the day in *Boumediene v. Bush*, guaranteeing Guantanamo Bay inmates *habeas corpus* rights, and in *Louisiana v. Kennedy*, limiting the death penalty to murder and crimes against the state. He also gave Justice Scalia a majority to invalidate the District of Columbia's broad ban on handguns and declare the Second Amendment's guarantee of individual rights to own them. He thus replicated a pattern he has established over his two decades on the high tribunal, leading more than one analyst to label the high tribunal "the Kennedy Court."[13]

The professorial justice's sense of humor is as quirky as his jurisprudence. He likes to start public lectures with a reference to the frustrations of modern travel. The joke's setup goes like this: "My wife and I recently returned from Europe, and, when we went to the baggage claim, our luggage was missing. When I reported the loss to the airline agent, he asked, 'Has your flight arrived?' 'No,' I replied, 'I am a mere shadow of my existential self!'" He has certainly cast a broad shadow, real or imagined, over the nation's highest court and its decisions.

To some observers, Kennedy evinces an infuriating inconsistency in his opinions. They say he twists in the wind until he fastens onto an idiosyncratic reason for deciding a case. To others, he is a thoughtful jurist who steadfastly refuses to embrace a results-oriented ideology; he simply analyzes each case on its own merits. Which assessment to apply may depend on the assessor's own ideological predilections. On one point, however, Anthony Kennedy's position is clear and unwavering: his commitment to the rule of law, the legal profession, the role of the judge, and the American constitutional cosmos.[14] Anyone who witnessed his compelling challenge to the United States to revitalize its civil society in the wake of the tragic 1995 bombing of the Alfred P. Murrah Federal Building in Oklahoma City, and after the 9/11 terrorist attacks in 2001, knows that his understanding of America's most admirable traditions is profound and indisputable.

CHAPTER FIVE

David H. Souter

An unlikely venue and occasion provide the perfect opportunity to view the public persona of David Souter, the man who was called the "stealth nominee" and "Justice Fuzzy" upon his appointment to the Supreme Court of the United States in 1990 because he was so little known in political and judicial circles at the time. In March 1996 Souter and his colleague Justice Anthony Kennedy appeared before a House of Representatives Appropriations Subcommittee, ostensibly to testify about the Court's budget for the next fiscal year. This now-annual ritual features some pro forma discussions of budget line items for the Court, and then members of the subcommittee turn to more substantive questions regarding the judiciary, which the justices answer with surprising frankness. Justice Souter, a slightly built man, attended the 1996 subcommittee hearing dressed in a pin-striped, charcoal-gray suit, starched white shirt, and sedate dark blue tie. At age fifty-seven, Souter wore his thinning, salt-and-pepper hair neatly trimmed. His face was marked by a perpetual five-o'clock shadow and revealed deep lines when he smiled. Deferring to his senior colleague, Souter referred to himself as "junior counsel" and declined when asked if he would like to add to Justice Kennedy's opening statement. After letting Kennedy answer most of the initial questions, Souter then made a few comments so that he would not appear to be "a bump on a log," as he put it. Self-deprecating humor, delivered in Souter's distinctive New England accent, has become one of his trademarks. Yet his twinkling eyes and benign facial expression turned as flinty as the granite hills of his beloved home state, New Hampshire, when the topics raised by the House committee struck a serious chord with him. Suddenly the terse Souter turned loquacious, even eloquent, defending the American jury system with raw passion as he described his early career as a prosecutor and then a trial judge, when he developed an admiration for jurors' abilities to comprehend complex arguments in criminal trials. And in relating a story about a stubborn grand jury, which refused to indict a suspect in a case Souter wanted to prosecute, he told of his eventual support for the "cantankerous" citizens who set themselves as counterpoints to the power of the state.

When the committee turned to its final topic of allowing television cameras in courtrooms, including the Supreme Court, Souter's response potently combined his dry humor, formidable character, and certainty of purpose: "The day you see a camera coming into our courtroom, it's gonna roll over my dead body!" He elaborated by saying that his experience with televised sessions at the New Hampshire Supreme Court, where he served seven years, proved to him that cameras have a detrimental effect on the judicial process. The 1996 hearing illustrated that six years after his appointment to the nation's highest court, Souter's personality and opinions were not in the least "fuzzy."[1]

Yet the 105th justice of the Supreme Court of the United States remains something of a mysterious paradox. Although he has followed the American pattern of many a small-town boy who made good, he has done so with a lifestyle that is *sui generis*. Born on September 17 (Constitution Day), 1939, in Melrose, Massachusetts, David Hackett Souter was the only child of Joseph Alexander and Helen Adams Hackett Souter. The Souters spent considerable time at the home of David's maternal grandparents in Weare, New Hampshire, a small, rural community just a few miles from Concord, the state capital. At age eleven, with his grandparents now deceased, young David and his parents moved to sedate Weare and settled in the ramshackle family farmhouse, a move necessitated by Joseph Souter's heart condition. David's father enjoyed the slower-paced life of a bank officer in Concord. Mr. Souter passed away in 1976 and Mrs. Souter eventually moved to a retirement home, but David Souter was still living in the family's Weare homestead when President George Bush plucked him from obscurity to place him on the nation's highest court in 1990. When his schedule allows time away from Washington, he continues to retreat to the secluded life of the small house that is stuffed with books, records, and memories.

By educational background alone, Souter seemed a worthy candidate for the U.S. Supreme Court. He attended public elementary schools and Concord High School, where he was elected president of the National Honor Society, served as coeditor of the yearbook and a reporter on the school newspaper, and was voted by his classmates as "most literary," "most sophisticated," and "most likely to succeed." One friend remembered, "He was very proper. He never swore. We were all trying to act macho; he never seemed to feel that need."[2] In fact, young David was so devout that he considered entering the Episcopal priesthood. His high school Latin teacher considered him a prodigy who could translate at the level of an advanced graduate student. Although bookish and quiet, he exhibited a trait that would last throughout his life—attracting a small but loyal circle of friends with his quick wit, warm charm, and caring nature.

Upon graduating in 1957 as salutatorian of the senior class, David entered Harvard College, where he joined the irreverent Hasty Pudding club and majored in philosophy, writing his senior honors thesis on the jurisprudence of Oliver Wendell Holmes. When he graduated *magna cum laude* and Phi Beta Kappa from Harvard in 1961, a group of his friends presented him with a scrapbook filled with headlines they had invented to represent the future they predicted for him: one read "David Souter Nominated to Supreme Court." Believing that he seemed destined for the prestigious judgeship, some of his friends took to calling him "Mr. Justice Souter."

The next step toward that destiny came with his selection as a Rhodes Scholar, which allowed him to attend Magdalen College at Oxford University to study law and philosophy for two years. His friends from that era remember that he accepted with ease the antiquated mores of the medieval university. His regular attendance at chapel set him apart from his Rhodes colleagues; and while they traveled in Europe during the long vacations, Souter stayed behind to study. When one of his friends did persuade him to tour the Continent, Souter played the archetypical Yankee, complaining that nothing in Europe compared favorably with his native New England. Other fellow Rhodes Scholars also recall that he was a staunch defender of the United States and was offended by anti-American comments. Still, he had already developed the high art of conversation and was considered an entertaining dinner companion, despite his preference for formality and privacy.

Like many Americans who study at Oxford, Souter earned a second bachelor's degree but distinguished himself by receiving on his exams in jurisprudence "a first," the highest commendation awarded by the prestigious university. After returning to the United States in 1963, Souter enrolled at Harvard Law School. A photograph from those years depicts young Souter dressed in a tuxedo and enjoying a cigar at a formal banquet. He performed well in his classes, though he did not try to upstage fellow students by volunteering answers at every opportunity. The future justice also did not serve on the law review, but one of his friends from law school believes that fact does not reflect any intellectual weakness. To the contrary, Souter's friend observes that he already possessed sterling credentials from Harvard College and a Rhodes Scholarship. Unlike some of his law school peers, he eschewed the cutthroat competition of students who had their eyes on the prizes of Supreme Court clerkships and New York law firms. His ever-present tie to New Hampshire was calling him back to his home state, he told friends.

Souter's proctorship of a Harvard freshman dormitory, where he was on call twenty-four hours a day, constituted a drain on his time but introduced him to problems unknown in his previously sheltered life. At his hearings before the Senate Judiciary Committee in 1990, Souter told the wrenching story of having to advise a freshman and his girlfriend after she became pregnant. The future justice did not reveal the nature of his advice to the distraught couple, but he used the event as an illustration of his exposure to the "real world." While attending law school, he dated Ellanor Stengel Fink, a student at Wheaton College, but neither the relationship with her nor his dating experiences with other women over the ensuing years resulted in marriage. Friends say that Souter is really wedded to the law and his career in it, following a pattern of working seven-day weeks during all of his professional life.

Graduating from Harvard in 1966, Souter returned to his beloved home in Weare and began his legal career in private practice with the firm of Orr & Reno in Concord. He found the general litigation practice there unrewarding and turned to the public sector. In 1968 he joined the staff of the New Hampshire attorney general as an assistant attorney general in the criminal division, with assignments at both the trial and appellate levels of the state court system. Warren Rudman, who was destined to become a U.S. senator and who would play a key role in supporting Souter's eventual U.S. Supreme Court nomination, became attorney general of New Hampshire in 1970 and promoted Souter to be his top aide as deputy attorney general. The two became close friends and professional colleagues. Rudman described Souter as the most talented member of his staff, with a skill for producing cogent, logical writing based on a thorough knowledge of case law. Moreover, the future senator was taken with Souter's warmth, good humor, and genuine concern for people. Rudman has reported that Souter's charm is especially attractive to children, with whom he communicates easily and genuinely. He is especially close to his goddaughter.

Rudman, upon resigning in 1976, persuaded Governor Meldrim Thomson to name Souter as his successor. In his two-year service as state attorney general, from 1976 to 1978, Souter personally argued several controversial religion cases. In one, he defended Governor Thomson's questionable order to fly the American and state flags at half-staff on Good Friday. He also supported in court the state's attempts to prosecute residents who, for religious reasons, covered up the state motto—"Live Free or Die"—on their license plates. The state was unsuccessful in the litigation of both cases.

Nevertheless, Souter's service was rewarded with a judicial appointment to the state Superior Court in 1978. He served on that trial court for five years, riding circuit around New Hampshire's ten counties, but usually trying cases in Concord and Manchester. He eventually encountered every kind of case that typically can come to a tribunal of general jurisdiction. His judicial reputation developed as fair but unsympathetic toward criminal defendants, and he acquired his admiration, expressed so eloquently at the 1996 congressional hearing, for juries. In 1983 New Hampshire Governor John Sununu, who would become President Bush's chief of staff, named Souter to the New Hampshire Supreme Court. On the five-person tribunal, Souter established himself as the intellectual leader and became a commanding presence at oral arguments. The high court of a small state tends not to hear cases of major constitutional import, but in a case challenging sobriety checkpoints, Souter dissented from his court's opinion that they were unconstitutional under the New Hampshire Constitution. Eventually, the U.S. Supreme Court agreed with Souter's point of view in upholding such checkpoints in a Michigan case (*Michigan Department of Transportation v. Sitz* [1990]).

Souter led a full and busy life outside the courtroom, however. He was a fixture at the local Episcopal church, where he assisted elderly parishioners. Inspired by a distant relative, Harriet Bartlett, whom he called "aunt" and who had a successful career as a medical social worker in Boston, he served on the Board of Trustees of Concord Hospital from 1972 to 1985, including a six-year stint as the board's president. In addition, he was an overseer of the Dartmouth Medical School, and he pursued his love of history as a trustee of the New Hampshire Historical Society. Although somewhat reclusive in his penchant for solitary pursuits, such as reading and listening to classical music, he also liked to escape to the outdoors and climb the White Mountains of his adopted state. By the time of his next promotion, Souter had become famous among his colleagues for his endearing preferences for driving dilapidated cars and eating the same lunch (yogurt or cottage cheese with a whole apple—core and all) day after day.

In 1987 the Senate refused to confirm President Ronald Reagan's nominee, Robert Bork, for a seat on the U.S. Supreme Court. Reagan's next nominee, Douglas Ginsburg, had to withdraw when word spread in the media that he had smoked marijuana. Senator Warren Rudman could hold his tongue no longer; he phoned Reagan's chief of staff, Howard Baker, and recommended David Souter for the still-vacant seat on the high court. White House aides spoke to Souter and were reportedly impressed, but Reagan nominated Californian Anthony Kennedy on the advice of his attorney general, Edwin Meese, who also hailed from the Golden State.

By early 1990 a position had opened on the U.S. First Circuit Court of Appeals, and Rudman was back on the phone with the White House, this time with George Bush's chief of staff, John Sununu, the former governor of New Hampshire who had placed Souter on the state Supreme Court. Bush nominated him to the First Circuit, and after brief Senate Judiciary Committee hearings, the Senate approved Souter's nomination unanimously. Judge Stephen Breyer, then chief judge of the First Circuit, swore him in on May 25, 1990. He had yet to write an opinion for that court when Justice William J. Brennan, Jr., unexpectedly announced his retirement from the Supreme Court on July 20, 1990. At age eighty-four Brennan was in declining health, but he had remained a vigorous member of the Court and a formidable creator of majority coalitions through its 1989–90 term. Indeed, he had fashioned majorities (albeit slim ones) for the dwindling liberal bloc in his last contentious cases involving flag-burning and affirmative action. Yet Justice Brennan, who had served with distinction since 1956, suffered a slight stroke early in the summer of 1990, and his physician urged him to accept the inevitable. He reluctantly announced his retirement, citing the incompatibility of the burdens of the Court with his fragile health.

Now Senator Rudman went to work to earn the ultimate prize for his friend and protégé. He phoned Sununu and then President Bush and told him, "Mr. President, you have just appointed this man [Souter] to the First Circuit Court of Appeals and he can easily be confirmed for the Supreme Court. I can guarantee you that he has no skeletons in his closet, and he's one of the most extraordinary human beings I've ever known."[3] Rudman then alerted his friend that the White House would probably contact him.

Bush was grateful for Rudman's recommendation but made no commitments to him over the phone. Nevertheless, the president publicly vowed to make quick work of the selection process for Brennan's replacement. The administration had compiled a list of potential nominees during Bush's first year in office; it included then-Solicitor General Kenneth Starr and three other federal appeals court judges (Edith Jones, Lawrence Silberman, and Clarence Thomas). White House Counsel C. Boyden Gray phoned Judge Souter at his Concord office on the weekend after Brennan announced he was leaving the Court and asked Souter to come to Washington on the very next day for a conversation with the president. Souter was skeptical of the process and his chances to land a nomination. Moreover, as he noted some years later, he was perfectly happy with his life in New Hampshire and thrilled to have been named to the U.S. Court of Appeals. Friends encouraged him to accept the request for an interview at the White House, if for no other reason than it would generate a lifetime's worth of interesting anecdotes. Souter acquiesced on the condition that he would answer no questions from the administration about his views on particular issues, especially abortion. A supportive Rudman drove Souter to the Manchester airport for his flight to Washington and even loaned his old friend $100 when the future justice discovered that he had only $3 in his wallet.

The short list of potential nominees had already been narrowed to Souter and Edith Jones by the time the former arrived at the White House to meet with administration staffers and the president himself. Bush and Souter had a productive discussion—two traditional New Englanders comparing notes and philosophies. In Souter, the president saw a perfect nominee for the times: a brilliant jurist who represented the best of American virtues while exhibiting no vices or known controversial positions on judicial issues. He had written over 200 opinions while on the New Hampshire Supreme Court, but they reflected a state docket rather than the divisive federal constitutional issues that reach the U.S. Supreme Court. A computer search of law-review articles turned up a sole example of Souter's published work, which consisted of a eulogy for a New Hampshire judge. If Robert Bork had been foiled by his own extensive paper trail of conservative commentaries on virtually every major constitutional debate of the day, Souter was indeed the "stealth nominee," named for the military aircraft whose unique design enables it to deflect radar. His very obscurity was the overwhelming deciding factor in his favor and gave him the nod over Judge Edith Jones.

With a stunned candidate at his side, President Bush announced Souter's nomination on the same day he met him for the first time, a mere seventy-two hours after Brennan had signaled his retirement from the bench. The president stressed that Souter was "a remarkable judge of keen intellect and the highest ability, one whose scholarly commitment to the law and whose wealth of experience mark him of first rank." Refusing to speculate on Souter's positions on specific issues, Bush tried to position him as a conservative with the coded language that Souter had "a keen appreciation of the proper judicial role rooted in fundamental belief in separation of powers and the democratic principles underlying our great system of government."[4] Bush's chief of staff, John Sununu, who as governor of New Hampshire had named Souter to the state's Supreme Court, remarked, "What [Souter] says and does is what he is. No pretense, no surprises."[5]

When called to the podium at the presidential news conference, Souter humbly thanked President Bush and then offered the media these few words, in rather jumbled syntax: "If it were possible for me to express to you the realization that I have of the honor which the president has just done me, I would try, and I would keep you here as long tonight as I had to do to get it out."[6] With that, he reserved any further comment for his confirmation hearings. Bush took a few more questions from reporters but successfully dodged all the inquiries calling for Souter's specific stance on issues. The news conference ended, and in the privacy of the White House Bush offered Souter a drink to calm him and called the nominee's mother to tell her the astonishing news. In the weeks leading up to his hearings before the Senate Judiciary Committee, Souter was subjected to media probes into his personal life that were painful for the nominee and fruitless for the journalists. For an intensely private man, the scouring of his life and habits (especially his bachelorhood) was nearly more than he could bear. In fact, he reportedly told his friend Senator Rudman that if he had known how vicious the process would be, he would not have let the senator propose his name.

Rudman defended the man he describes as being like a "very special younger brother" to him. Introducing Souter on the first day of hearings before the Senate Judiciary Committee, Rudman angrily declared, "It is remarkable that there are some people here in Washington who view a man who has a single-minded dedication to his chosen profession, the law, and possesses great qualities of humility, graciousness, frugality, charity, reverence to his faith and to his family is somehow regarded as an anomaly and somehow out of touch with life."[7] Rudman later wrote, "If David Souter is odd, our society is in big trouble."[8] But Rudman need not have worried; his old friend from New Hampshire impressed the committee with the very qualities Rudman had always admired in him. Souter's nomination cleared the Judiciary Committee by a vote of 13-1, with only Senator Edward Kennedy (D.-Mass.) casting a negative vote. The full Senate was equally favorable, approving Souter by a vote of 90-9. The new justice was sworn in on October 9, 1990, and began work almost immediately on the fall term, which was already underway.

During his entire first term on the high bench, Justice Souter was inundated with the work that awaited him in an atmosphere, in a city and a context that were totally unfamiliar to him. He described the burdensome work that he faced on the high court as "walking through a tidal wave."[9] Historically, freshmen justices take a reserved role while they acclimate to their new surroundings, but Souter was even less visible than most. He wrote only eight majority opinions, none of which was considered of major significance, and penned just two concurring and two dissenting opinions. His votes aligned him with the Court's conservative bloc, but he had the highest level of agreement (89 percent) with Justice Sandra Day O'Connor, considered a moderate conservative.[10] In criminal justice cases, he continued his tendency from his days on the New Hampshire courts to side with the government as opposed to defendants. Observers noted that his predecessor, Justice Brennan, a champion of criminal rights, would surely have voted in the opposite direction from his replacement. Conservatives also hailed Souter's decisive vote in *Rust v. Sullivan*, which upheld the constitutionality of regulations prohibiting federally funded family planning clinics from discussing abortion with their clients.

After a refreshing summer in Weare, Souter returned to the Court for his second term in the fall of 1991 with much more confidence in his ability to handle the job at an institution he utterly revered. His charm, warmth, and good humor had won him friends among the Court's close-knit staff. He settled into a routine in his chambers, where, perhaps to recall his roots, he hung a portrait of Harlan Fiske Stone (also from New Hampshire), who had served as associate justice and then chief justice earlier in the century. Visitors to Souter's office have noted that it is unusually dark, with no desk lamps to cast additional light, and, reflecting the justice's traditional work habits, he writes in calligraphic longhand rather than succumb to the modern convenience of a computer. Souter also settled into a routine in oral arguments, often asking probing but polite questions of counsel. Once, at a 1994 oral argument, his strong New England brogue betrayed him. He was attempting to ask a counsel about the "flaw" in his argument. It was a reasonable question, to be sure, except that with Souter's accent, the question asked for the "floor" in the attorney's contention. The baffled counsel paused and then wisely asked for a clarification on Souter's query regarding the "floor" in his position. The justice realized the source of confusion and then sheepishly apologized for what he called his "regional accent," prompting laughter from those assembled in the courtroom.

After arriving at the Court, Justice Souter struck up a friendship with his predecessor, the retired Justice Brennan, who maintained chambers in the Court building. A poignant photograph of the two shows Justice Souter tenderly supporting a feeble Justice Brennan by the arm as they attended the 1993 funeral of Justice Thurgood Marshall. We may never know the extent of Justice Brennan's jurisprudential influence on his successor, but Justice Souter's moving eulogy to his friend "Bill" at the latter's funeral in 1997 spoke volumes about their close personal relationship. The reserved, formal Yankee judge revealed how the gregarious Irish jurist would embrace him in a warm bear hug, call him "pal," and always make him feel "great" during visits to his chambers. Tongue in cheek, Justice Souter also reminisced about how Justice Brennan, a renowned master at mustering majorities on the nine-person Court, taught him "how to count to five."[11]

The majority that Souter helped fashion in the 1992 case of *Planned Parenthood of Pennsylvania v. Casey* was reminiscent of Brennan-led factions in the past. Holding the votes of *Roe v. Wade*'s author, Justice Harry Blackmun, and Justice John Paul Stevens for part of the decision, Souter was influential in coauthoring a plurality opinion with Justices O'Connor and Kennedy that reaffirmed what the trio called the "central holding" of *Roe*, that a woman may choose to terminate her pregnancy based on the prerogative of a constitutionally protected personal liberty. The three centrist justices argued that the 1973 *Roe* precedent was such an accepted part of society in 1992 that the Court should protect the core of the ruling and its own legitimacy by reaffirming the heart of the decision. Souter, Kennedy, and O'Connor abandoned *Roe*'s trimester system of determining when a woman had an unfettered right to choose an abortion, however, and substituted the "undue burden" test for it. A state limitation on access to abortion poses such a burden, in the plurality's definition, when it "has the purpose and effect of placing a substantial obstacle in the path of a woman seeking an abortion of a nonviable fetus."[12]

Needless to relate, conservatives, particularly members of the pro-life movement, were devastated that Souter had not provided the fifth vote to overturn *Roe v. Wade*. He would not do so in two other cases involving bans on so-called partial-birth abortions. *Stenberg v. Carhart* (2000) found Souter with the five-justice majority striking down Nebraska's ban. In 2007, however, Souter's vote to invalidate the federal prohibition on partial-birth procedures placed him in the minority (*Gonzales v. Carhart*). Justice Samuel Alito's replacement of Justice O'Connor in 2006 added a pro-life vote to the high bench.

The "stealth nominee" from New Hampshire, who was supposed to offer "no surprises," did not shy away from an escalated war of words with his conservative colleague Antonin Scalia, with whom he has sparred in several opinions.[13] In First Amendment Establishment Clause cases, Souter began to take the lead on the separationist side. He wrote for the Court in *Board of Education of Kiryas Joel School District v. Grumet* that the state of New York could not constitutionally carve out a separate school district for a village of Satmar Hasidic Jews so that they would not have to send their special-education/handicapped students to secular public schools. Scalia's dissent in the 1994 case repeatedly criticized Souter by name, violating the Court's long-standing tradition of not singling out individual justices for reproach (especially when they are representing the Court as an institution in a majority opinion). Souter's passionate dissent in *Rosenberger v. University of Virginia* (1995) also argued the separationist cause by defending the university's decision not to fund a student-run Christian magazine with proceeds from a student activities fee. He authored another vehement dissent, this time in 2002's *Zelman v. Simmons-Harris*, from Chief Justice William Rehnquist's 5-4 decision in favor of government vouchers that provided tuition aid for needy students in Cleveland to attend private schools of their parents' choice. Parents receiving the vouchers chose Catholic schools 95 percent of the time. Souter accused the majority of promoting "divisiveness" through its "dramatic departure from basic Establishment Clause principles."[14]

In school prayer cases, Souter again supported a high wall between church and state. He contributed a strong concurrence with Justice Kennedy's majority opinion to prohibit clergy-led prayers at public school graduations in *Lee v. Weisman* (1992) and voted with the majority's ruling in *Santa Fe School District v. Doe* (2000) banning student prayer over the public address system at public school football games in Texas. Not long after the latter, Souter explained his vote to a group of high school students in Washington, "Although I am a religious person, I do not favor prayer at games because eliminating it doesn't prevent individuals from praying. When I was in school, I never had official prayer before math class, but I can assure you, I prayed before each and every math class."[15]

Souter reflected an equally staunch separationist position regarding religious displays in public buildings. He penned the Court's opinion in *McCreary County v. American Civil Liberties Union* (2005), arguing that two Kentucky counties' displays of the Ten Commandments in their courthouses served a religious purpose and, therefore, violated the Establishment Clause. On the same day, the Court handed down *Van Orden v. Perry*, upholding the display of the Decalogue on Texas's capitol grounds. Justice Stephen Breyer provided the crucial fifth vote in *Van Orden*. For him the fact that the Fraternal Order of Eagles had donated the granite depiction of the Ten Commandments in 1962, and that no one had complained about it during the four decades of its existence, were determinative.

Under the Free Exercise Clause of the First Amendment, Souter wrote a con-currence in the 1993 case of *Church of the Lukumi Babalu Aye v. Hialeah*, agreeing with the Court's ruling in favor of striking down a Hialeah law against animal sacrifice practiced by the Cuban American Santeria sect. But Souter added that the Court should return to its previously more liberal test for upholding free-exercise claims in virtually all cases. Thus, he was in dissent from the Court's 1997 ruling in *City of Boerne v. Flores* overturning the Religious Freedom Restora-tion Act, which was Congress's attempt to force the Court to do just what he had argued in *Hialeah*.

By the 1994–95 term, when the second Clinton appointee, Justice Breyer, joined the Court, Souter could most often be found in civil rights and liberties cases aligning with the more liberal wing of the Court. Because that wing usually consisted of a four-person minority (Souter, Stevens, Ginsburg, and Breyer), Souter was frequently in dissent, as he was in two 1995 race cases, *Adarand v. Peña* and *Missouri v. Jenkins II*, where the Court reached a conservative outcome. In majority-minority districting cases, concerning voting districts created on the basis of race to ensure minority representation, he was again on the losing side, supporting such race-based reapportionment remedies throughout the 1990s. He contributed a vote to the winning position, however, in *Grutter v. Bollinger*, the 2003 case that sanctioned using race and ethnicity as "plus" factors in the University of Michigan Law School's affirmative action policy.

Souter dissented in federalism cases, where the Rehnquist Court made its mark siding with state power. In *U.S. v. Lopez* (1995) and *Printz v. United States* (1997), the Court's more conservative majority struck down congressional exercises in gun control as overstepping the bounds of federal power. Leading the dissenters in *U.S. v. Morrison* (2000), Souter supported the federal Violence Against Women Act of 1994 as a valid exercise of Congress's authority to regulate interstate commerce. In another gender case, *Faragher v. City of Boca Raton* (1998), he produced the majority opinion in which the Court held that an employer is vicariously liable for actionable sexual harassment caused by a supervisor, but subject to an affirmative defense looking to the reasonableness of the employer's conduct as well as that of the victim.

Though Souter's votes continued their liberal trend, he occasionally returned to his more conservative roots, particularly in criminal justice cases. One of his majority opinions, delivered for the Court in the search and seizure ruling, *Atwater v. City of Lago Vista* (2001), seemed particularly harsh and drew criticism from Justice O'Connor's dissent. Souter wrote for the 5–4 majority that the

Fourth Amendment does not forbid warrantless arrests for minor criminal offenses, in this instance a misdemeanor seatbelt violation punishable only by a fine. What raised O'Connor's ire was the fact that Lago Vista, Texas, police had hauled Atwater off to jail in front of her two frightened young children because no one in her car was wearing a seatbelt.

Bush v. Gore, the historic case that effectively determined the winner of the 2000 presidential race, placed Souter and Breyer between two blocs on the high Court. The pair agreed with the more conservative majority that the standardless recounts of votes in Florida violated the Fourteenth Amendment's Equal Protection Clause. Whereas the Court's conservatives had five votes to stop the recount, Souter and Breyer thought that Florida could develop constitutional procedures for continuing to count ballots. John Paul Stevens and Ruth Bader Ginsburg were in complete dissent, observing no equal protection violations. A photo of Justice Souter driving away from the Court the day *Bush v. Gore* came down reveals a dour, bleary-eyed visage. Some reports indicated that the divisive decision so upset him that he considered resigning from the bench.[16] As if the slings and arrows of judicial battles were not enough, Souter suffered minor injuries when a group of thugs attacked him while he jogged near his Washington apartment in spring 2004.

By the time the 2008 presidential election approached, Souter again considered retiring but only if the Democrats won the presidency. His frugal Yankee lifestyle and investment in a New Hampshire bank that soared to over $5 million assure a financially comfortable retirement. Siding with the liberal justices, Stevens, Ginsburg, and Breyer, more than three-quarters of the time meant that Souter often found himself among the dissenters, especially in 2006–07, when many of the high-profile civil rights and liberties cases resulted in conservative outcomes. Whether frustrations over the dwindling influence of his judicial positions will cause him to return to the peace and solitude of his beloved New Hampshire home remains to be seen. While continuing to fly under the radar in his personal life, eshewing the social whirl of official Washington, Justice David Souter has made his mark on American constitutional law. He is most assuredly no longer the "stealth justice."

CHAPTER SIX

Clarence Thomas

Clarence Thomas has observed that biographers can portray their subjects as saints or devils, but they can never peer into their souls and know what life was really like for them. Such is the challenge for anyone chronicling the biography of the second African American to sit on the Supreme Court of the United States. Yet Thomas frequently speaks publicly, and has written extensively, of the triumphs and tragedies in his life's story and how he reacted to them. He remembers his youth, when he "was just a little black kid in a world that is far away—both in space and time" from the world he inhabits now, "cloistered in the judiciary."[1]

Indeed, Thomas's ascendance to the highest tribunal in the land could never have been predicted from the dire circumstances of his birth and early childhood years. The progeny of West African slaves who worked the plantations of Georgia's low country, he was born on June 23, 1948, just south of Savannah, in a poverty-stricken segregated community called Pinpoint. The marshy settlement of no more than 100 black residents perched on a twenty-five acre peninsula, surrounded by Shipyard Creek. In the twentieth century, slave descendants eked out a bare subsistence there by catching and processing shellfish or serving as laborers for nearby white homeowners.

Clarence was the second of three children (he had an older sister and a younger brother) born to Leola ("Pigeon") Williams and M.C. Thomas. For the first seven years of his life, the future justice lived in a shanty, lit by kerosene lamps, with no indoor plumbing. In the winter, the family had to stuff old newspapers in the wall's chinks to try to ward off the cold. When he was two years old, his father abandoned the family, leaving his mother with two children and a third one on the way. She attempted to support her family by working as a maid and obtaining clothes for her children from their Baptist church's clothing drives. Despite these privations, Thomas describes his early childhood as "idyllic." He loved exploring the marshes and woods that constituted Pinpoint. He was just as excited to enroll in Haven Home School, a segregated elementary school, to which he and his older sister took a school bus each day.

At the age of six, Clarence walked home from the bus stop to discover that his little brother and cousin had accidentally burned down their substandard home. Pigeon sent Clarence's sister to live with relatives and took her two boys to Savannah, where they lived in even worse conditions than they had known in Pinpoint. Their new home consisted of a one-room apartment in a squalid urban tenement. The filthy outhouse was surrounded by a broken pipe that poured raw sewage into the backyard. Young Clarence had to sleep in a small chair while his mother and younger brother used the only bed in the apartment. The future justice continued first grade at another segregated school, but the uninspired lessons prompted him to cut classes and wander the ghetto streets surrounding his new home. Winters were cold in the dilapidated apartment and, unlike in Pinpoint, where fresh fish and vegetables were abundant, the Thomases had little to eat in the city, as Pigeon struggled to make ends meet from her meager domestic's wages of $10 per week. After moving to a slightly better apartment, she finally gave up and sent her two boys to live with their grandfather, Myers Anderson, and his wife Christine in a modest but nice home he had built on a well-kept Savannah street. Clarence and his brother arrived with all of their possessions in two grocery bags. Their grandfather, whom they would call "Daddy," announced, "The damn vacation's over!" He immediately set about molding two responsible young men through a strict regimen of manual labor and object lessons. When Clarence complained about the amount of work he and his brother were expected to perform, telling Daddy, "Slavery's over!," their new father figure retorted, "Not in my damn house!"[2]

Anderson, a devout Catholic, an active member of the NAACP, and a resourceful businessman (he was a self-employed deliverer of fuel and ice), sent Thomas to a parochial school, St. Benedict the Moor, which was staffed by strict but supportive nuns. Although the school was racially segregated, Thomas notes that its emphasis on discipline and achievement was determinative in his life. He never fails to acknowledge and thank the nuns who taught him there, and he invited them to his investitures for both the U.S. Court of Appeals and the U.S. Supreme Court. Thomas also credits his grandparents with instilling in him good manners and respectful behavior. He recalls that "any report that we threw trash on the ground, failed to greet an adult properly, or engaged in any improper behavior resulted in immediate sanctions."[3] Other institutions, like the local library, nourished his love of reading and helped him to escape into an imaginary world far from the strictures of the Jim Crow South in the 1950s. In later years Thomas has grieved over the loss of what he calls the "ameliorating structures" of his old neighborhood. The small businesses are gone, having succumbed to urban decay; his Catholic elementary school is closed, its convent tellingly converted to a halfway house; and the branch library stands empty.

In 1964 Thomas, who had embraced Catholicism wholeheartedly, withdrew from his segregated parochial high school, to enroll in a nearly all-white Catholic boarding school, St. John Vianny Minor Seminary, in Savannah. His grandfather, noting the steep tuition of $400 per year, counseled Thomas, "You can't quit. Don't shame me and don't shame our race."[4] Although subject to the racist attitudes of some of his classmates, Thomas made excellent grades, worked on the yearbook, and enjoyed playing sports. He attended classes six days a week, after awakening at 6 A.M. to attend chapel, and retired by 9 P.M. each night. One day the seminary's rector told Thomas that his spoken English was substandard. The teenager felt demeaned by what he assumed was a racist attack on his accent, but many years later he discovered that the rector had made similar comments to white students. Thomas was so hurt and angry that he vowed to rid his speech of Gullah, a mix of southern and African dialects native to the black inhabitants of the Sea Islands off the Carolina and Georgia coasts.

After Clarence's graduation from high school in 1967, Grandfather Anderson sent him to Immaculate Conception Seminary in northwestern Missouri to continue his study toward the priesthood, though the young man was having second thoughts about his religious vocation. Thomas was not the only black student there, but he suffered from the poor race relations extant at the school. He wondered why the Catholic Church failed to take a public stand against racism in the midst of the Civil Rights Movement. A bigoted, insensitive remark by a fellow student about the assassination of Martin Luther King, Jr., in April 1968 confirmed Thomas's doubts: he would *not* become a priest.

The decision bitterly disappointed his grandfather, who promptly kicked him out of the house. Clarence eventually enrolled at the College of the Holy Cross in Worcester, Massachusetts, which had begun an active recruitment program for minority students. Thomas was a devoted student who "was always in the library," according to one friend. He majored in English literature to obliterate the vestiges of his childhood dialect. He recalls that he did not necessarily want to major in English but thought it essential to do so in order to learn how to speak and write properly.

Despite his devotion to studies, Thomas found time to work in the school cafeteria, become a resident assistant for the all-black corridor in one of the dorms, volunteer to help the poor in Worcester, and engage in student protests. He also assisted in founding the Black Student Union at Holy Cross. He considered the Black Power Movement inspiring and adopted the clothing and hairstyle of its radical leaders. Thomas seemed haunted by racial isolation (he was one of only six blacks in his class) and seriously considered dropping out of college. Yet, fearful that he would be drafted for service in the Vietnam War, Thomas stayed at Holy Cross and graduated ninth in his class in 1971 with honors in English. Another reason that Thomas may have decided to stay in school was his introduction to Kathy Ambush, a pretty coed at a nearby Catholic women's college. A few days after they met, Thomas told a friend that he was in love with Kathy, and they were married in Worcester the day after Clarence's college commencement. Their son Jamal was born two years later.

By his senior year, Thomas had decided to become a lawyer and applied to Harvard. Its prestigious law school accepted him, but he felt uncomfortable with its large size and conservatism. Thomas won admission to Yale University Law School through its affirmative action program and decided to enroll because it was smaller and more liberal than Harvard. In his courses, he received mostly passes on Yale's grading scale of honors, pass, low pass, and fail. Feelings of "rage" and loneliness overtook him when whites snubbed him as an affirmative action token and blacks with more elite backgrounds ignored him. In his third year of law school he interviewed with law firms but again felt he was treated differently because of his race. He had hoped to return to his home state of Georgia to work against the injustices he had witnessed in his childhood but was rebuffed by the major law firms there. He still recalls the bitterness that welled up inside him at the time when all he had to show for his efforts were the "barren husks of rejection letter after rejection letter."[5] He thought his Yale law degree so worthless that he stuck a fifteen-cent sticker on its frame and, to this day, stores it in his basement, rather than display it proudly in his Supreme Court chambers.

Rescuing him from his frustration and despair after law school was a young, charismatic lawyer and politician, John C. Danforth. Then attorney general of Missouri, Danforth offered Thomas a position in his office as an assistant attorney general. The fact that Thomas at the time was not a Republican and had even voted for George McGovern, the hapless Democratic candidate for president in 1972, did not matter to Danforth, a rising star in the Republican Party. After his graduation from Yale in 1974, Thomas passed the Missouri bar and began putting in long hours in the attorney general's office. He describes those years as ones of continued economic hardship, as he struggled to make ends meet while supporting his wife and young son. One morning, while walking to work, he discovered a wallet, stuffed with bills totaling over $600—representing more than his monthly take-home pay. He wrestled with his conscience over what to do with the windfall but ultimately returned the lost billfold to its rightful owner, knowing that the moral lessons dictated by his scrupulous grandparents required that he do so. His honesty went unrewarded by the wallet's white owner, who treated Thomas with suspicion and ingratitude.

With Danforth's election to the Senate in 1977, Thomas took a job as an attorney with the Monsanto Company, a chemical manufacturer in St. Louis. His duties included ensuring that pesticides produced by the company met federal guidelines. In 1979 he moved to Washington, D.C., and became a legislative assistant to Senator Danforth on the condition that he *not* be assigned to civil rights issues. His resentment toward the tokenism of affirmative action, bred during his days at Yale, combined with his grandfather's lessons on self-sufficiency and independence, had moved Thomas into a small circle of black conservatives who rejected the dependency allegedly fostered among blacks by the welfare state. He registered as a Republican and voted for Ronald Reagan in the 1980 presidential election.

Thomas's conservative ideas quickly brought him to the attention of the Reagan administration, which was always looking for qualified conservative minorities. In 1981 Thomas was appointed assistant secretary for civil rights in the United States Department of Education. He openly stated that minorities must succeed by their own merit and that affirmative action programs and civil rights legislation do not improve living standards. In 1982 he became the chairman of the United States Equal Employment Opportunity Commission, which was designed to enforce antidiscrimination laws that cover race, gender, and age in the workplace. Thomas served two consecutive terms as chairman, despite having previously sworn that he would never work at the EEOC. Over his eight-year tenure there, Thomas shifted the focus of the commission from large class action law suits to individual cases of discrimination.

Yet as Thomas's professional career rocketed upward, his personal life was disintegrating, and he was drowning his sorrows in alcohol. His wife Kathy and he separated in 1981 and were divorced in 1984. Thomas was granted custody of his son. In 1983, his beloved grandfather died, plunging Thomas into grief over years wasted before they had reconciled shortly before Daddy passed away. Fleeting thoughts of suicide even crossed his mind, but he did not want to abandon his son as his biological father had abandoned him.

Three years after reaching the depths of despair, Thomas met Virginia Lamp, a lobbyist for the U.S. Chamber of Commerce, at a conference. They were married five months later, with Jamal serving as best man for his father at the ceremony. Now married over two decades, he introduces his wife Virginia at public events as the "most wonderful human being in the world" and his "best friend."

In 1990 President George Bush appointed Thomas to the U.S. Court of Appeals for the Washington, D.C. Circuit, a well-known professional stepping stone to the Supreme Court. Thomas filled the seat left vacant by the resignation of Robert Bork, the unsuccessful nominee to the Supreme Court in 1987. In Thomas's brief eighteen-month stint on the appeals court, he wrote only twenty opinions, none of which involved major constitutional issues. He also voted but did not contribute written opinions in approximately sixty decisions. Hewing to a clear conservative line, Thomas tended to defer to the government in cases brought by all parties except businesses. Thus, litigants with civil and criminal rights appeals, challenges under environmental laws, antitrust enforcement cases, and labor grievances generally found an unsympathetic ear in Judge Thomas.[6]

In June 1991 an aging, frail Thurgood Marshall announced his retirement from the Supreme Court, where he had served as the tribunal's first and only black member since his historic appointment by President Lyndon Johnson in 1967. President George Bush faced a thorny political dilemma in choosing Marshall's successor. African Americans saw the Marshall position on the Court as the "black seat," in the tradition of seats reserved for Catholics, Jews, and geographic constituencies in the past. Yet Bush had voiced his opposition to racial quotas in employment and education, so he could hardly nominate a justice solely because of his or her race. In addition, he had riled the conservative wing of his party by failing to continue the Reagan legacy in many policy areas; therefore, he could ill afford to widen the chasm by nominating a politically moderate, let alone a liberal, minority.

In anticipation of the departure of either Marshall or Justice Harry Blackmun, both of whom were octogenarians, Bush's advisers had composed lists of possible nominees. When Marshall preceded Blackmun in retirement, the Bush administration placed a heavy emphasis on minority and women candidates. Joining several Hispanic, and two women, federal judges on the list was Clarence Thomas, who clearly was being groomed for the appointment by his elevation to the

U.S. Court of Appeals in Washington. Moreover, Thomas's publicly articulated conservative stands on some of the most contentious issues on the country's judicial agenda, combined with his age (he was just forty-three), made him a most attractive possibility. At the urging of Vice President Dan Quayle and White House Counsel C. Boyden Gray, President Bush had winnowed his choices to Thomas and asked him to the Bush summer home in Kennebunkport, Maine, for a meeting on July 1. The president presented Thomas with two questions as they chatted in Bush's bedroom: "If you are appointed to the [Supreme] Court, could you call them as you see them?" When Thomas assured him that he could, the president queried, "Can you and your family make it through the confirmation process?" Thomas observed that he had successfully navigated four confirmation processes in the previous decade. Bush assured the federal judge that he would never publicly criticize any decisions he might make on the highest court in the land. Then the president told Thomas,"At two o'clock, I will announce that I will appoint you to the Supreme Court. Now let's go and have lunch."[7] The flabber-gasted Thomas was so stunned that he had trouble rising from his chair, but he made a call to his wife to calm himself. In proclaiming his choice to replace Thurgood Marshall, Bush argued that "the fact that he [Thomas] is black has nothing to do with the sense that he is the best qualified at this time."[8] ("Even I had my doubts about so extravagant a claim," Thomas recalled years later.[9]) The new nominee then stepped to the microphone to proclaim the improbability of his appointment that he could never have dreamed of as a child and to thank, with a catch in his voice, his grandparents, mother, and the nuns who taught him that he could rise above his lowly birth.

Throughout the confirmation process, the president would repeat the claim that Thomas's race had nothing to do with his appointment, in an unsuccessful attempt to protect Bush's reputation as an opponent of racial quotas. Very few students of the Court believed that Thomas, with his limited experience, would have been chosen had he been white. The American Bar Association's Committee on Judiciary confirmed this view when it subsequently rated him as merely "Qualified," because of his lack of legal credentials. Nonetheless, as Thomas humbly and poignantly accepted the nomination on the lawn outside Bush's tony Kennebunkport summer estate on a sunny New England afternoon, neither he nor the president could have imagined just how stormy the confirmation process would become.

Civil rights interest groups portrayed varied reactions to the Thomas nomina-tion. The NAACP's board was nearly unanimous in its 49–1 vote against the appointment of Thomas, whom they accused of being oblivious to institutional racism in his opposition to affirmative action and welfare policies. The National Bar Association (a group of black attorneys) narrowly opposed the Thomas nomination. The National Urban League decided to express its neutrality on the appointment, and the National Council of Black Lawyers, a liberal interest group, announced their opposition to Thomas's promotion to the Supreme Court. Only the Southern Christian Leadership Conference, among the major civil rights organizations, supported him.

After an undistinguished hearing before the Senate Judiciary Committee, during which Thomas refused to be drawn into lengthy discussions of his conservative record and writings, the Committee tied 7-7 in its vote on the nominee, and his name headed to the full Senate without the endorsement of the committee. Before the Senate's vote, however, journalists leaked a sensational story about an FBI report that the Judiciary Committee had received in which University of Oklahoma law professor Anita Hill accused Thomas of sexually harassing her when she worked at the EEOC. The committee summoned Hill, an African-American graduate of Yale Law School, who described in shocking detail the nature of the alleged harassment in front of a transfixed, national television audience of 20 million households. The nominee was recalled to respond to the charges, which he denied absolutely with obvious contempt for the process that he described as "a high-tech lynching for uppity blacks," evoking the fatal end that many black men met in the South before antilynching laws went into effect. Despite the improbable spectacle, Thomas was approved by the Senate 52-48, the closest Supreme Court confirmation vote of the twentieth century. When his wife reported to Thomas that he had been confirmed, the disgusted appointee replied, "Whoop-dee damn-doo."[10] Seven years after his humiliating ordeal, Justice Thomas still spoke of it in bitter terms, describing the Hill hearings as "just a plain whipping" from which he still had not fully healed.[11] In 2007 he told a 60 Minutes television audience that liberals orchestrated the confirmation attack on his character because they feared he would vote to overturn abortion rights.

The political atmosphere turned so poisonous after Thomas's confirmation that U.S. marshals who were guarding him advised the appointee to wear a bullet-proof vest. On October 23, 1991, an emotionally battered but determined Clarence Thomas was sworn in as an associate justice of the Supreme Court in a ceremony on the White House lawn. Even the new justice's biological father appeared for this triumphant celebration in his son's life. Justice Thomas has admitted that he was not a student of the Court before he began serving on it. In fact, he had never attended an oral argument session at the high court. His biggest surprise upon arriving at the imposing building was how civil and respectful his fellow justices were toward him. Justice Byron White bolstered him by saying, "It doesn't matter how you got here. All that matters now is what you do here."[12] Although he has described the workload as "voracious" and challenging, and claims that it took several years for him to feel completely comfortable with it, Justice Thomas embraced a relatively visible role in opinion writing from the beginning. Not surprisingly, he quickly settled into a voting bloc that included his conservative soulmates Justice Antonin Scalia and Chief Justice William Rehnquist. In the 1997–98 term, for example, Thomas and Scalia voted together 82 percent of the time in non-unanimous cases. A decade later, in the 2006–07 term, the two conservative justices were still in agreement in four-fifths of the rulings. That same term, Thomas and Scalia joined with their new conservative colleagues, Chief Justice Roberts and Justice Samuel Alito, to win over half of the 24 cases decided by 5–4 votes, by attracting swing justice Anthony Kennedy. Journalist Jan Crawford Greenburg has argued that documentary evidence available in Justice Harry Blackmun's papers at the Library of Congress dispels the long-held myth that Thomas has been Scalia's "lackey." Conversely, she discovered that Thomas often attracted Scalia to his arguments.

Thomas is remarkably silent in oral argument, sometimes sitting through entire terms of the Court without posing a single question to the counsel arguing before the bench. At most, he asks but a handful of queries per term. He traces his reticence to advice imparted by his grandparents: "My grandmother told me, 'You can't talk and listen at the same time.' If I wanted to talk a lot, I'd be on the other side of the bench."[13] He also cites the fact that he has read all of the briefs in the cases being argued, and he genuinely wants to hear the oral statements from the attorneys. In addition, he notes that he still carries the stigma of his Gullah dialect (though to the untrained ear it is undetectable). Thomas told an appreciative gathering of the conservative Federalist Society in 2007, "One thing I've demonstrated in 16 years [on the Supreme Court] is you can do this job without asking a single question."[14]

In general, the civil rights community was correct in predicting that Thomas would often oppose their interests. His unwillingness to interpret broadly the Constitution or statutes clearly applies to matters of race. In the 1992 case of *Presley v. Etowah County Commission*, he joined the majority in holding that the Voting Rights Act of 1965 did not forbid two Alabama counties to change their systems of road management in such a way that they reduced the effective power of newly elected black commissioners. Similarly, he sided with the Court in 1993's *Shaw v. Reno* decision, holding that state officials must present a "compelling" reason to justify "bizarre" congressional districts drawn to contain a majority of blacks or Hispanics. One year later, concurring in *Holder v. Hall*, he urged passionately that the Voting Rights Act does not require, nor could it constitutionally, that race be considered affirmatively in districting. When *Shaw's* progeny arrived at the Court in 1994-95, Thomas again voted with the majority, this time ruling in *Miller v. Johnson* that when race is the "predominant factor" in establishing legislative districts, they should be presumed unconstitutional.

Thomas's most controversial opinions in race cases came at the end of the 1994-95 term. In *Missouri v. Jenkins II* the justices ruled by a 5-4 majority that a federal judge had improperly attempted to integrate the public schools of Kansas City, Missouri, by ordering massive expenditures in an attempt to attract students from surrounding suburbs. Thomas's stunningly emotive concurring opinion declared, "It never ceases to amaze me that the courts are so willing to assume that anything that is predominantly black must be inferior."[15] The same day as the Court handed down *Jenkins*, it announced its opinion in *Adarand v. Peña*, which determined that judges must apply "strict scrutiny" to federal affirmative action programs, thus jeopardizing all such plans. Not surprisingly, given his previous record against affirmative action as a remedial public policy, Thomas voted with the narrow 5-4 majority. He also joined Justice Scalia's concurrence, which went beyond Justice O'Connor's more moderate controlling opinion, to declare that the government can *never* constitutionally justify racial discrimination against whites as a remedy for past discrimination against minorities.[16]

When the issue of affirmative action in higher education arrived at the Court for the first time since 1978, via the 2003 University of Michigan cases, Thomas finally had his chance to vote against the race-based policies he so abhors. He did so in both the law school (*Grutter v. Bollinger*) and undergraduate (*Gratz v. Bollinger*) cases. His *Grutter* dissent reflected bitterness and anger that Justice O'Connor had marshaled a majority to uphold the use of race and ethnicity as a "plus" factor in admissions to the UM Law School. Wrote Thomas, "Like [Frederick] Douglass, I believe that blacks can achieve in every avenue of American life without the meddling of university administrators."[17] Not surprisingly, he voted with the majority in the 2007 Louisville and Seattle rulings that banned the use of race in assigning students to public schools to ensure diversity.

In one of his first criminal rights cases on the Supreme Court, Thomas followed the tendency he manifested on the Court of Appeals in siding against an inmate who argued that a prison guard had used excessive force against him and thus violated his Eighth Amendment right against cruel and unusual punishment. In dissent from the Court's 1992 opinion in *Hudson v. McMillian*, Thomas argued that the guarantees of Amendment VIII should not, by judicial fiat, be codified to regulate the behavior of prison authorities throughout the country. His opinion seemed especially ironic in light of his comment at the first set of his 1991 confirmation hearings that he would gaze out his window at prisoners coming to the courthouse in Washington and think to himself, "There but for the grace of God go I." Yet Thomas wrote for a unanimous Court in the 1995 case *Wilson v. Arkansas* that the Fourth Amendment's proscription of unreasonable government searches and seizures may be triggered by a police officer's unannounced entry into a home. Per Thomas's opinion, the Court accepted the common law principle that law enforcers should knock and announce their presence before bursting into a suspect's home. Nevertheless, Thomas left it to lower courts to determine exceptions to the common law rule when countervailing law enforcement considerations might prevail. But Thomas returned to his hard line against the aggrieved individual in the Court's 1997 5–4 decision in *Kansas v. Hendricks*, which upheld the state's Sexually Violent Predator Act. Thomas argued for the Court that the act's procedures for civil commitment and its definition of "mental abnormality" in the context of violent pedophilia satisfied "substantive" due process requirements.

In two criminal rights cases handed down at the end of the 1997–98 term, Justice Thomas authored both majority opinions for closely split decisions. He joined the more liberal justices—Souter, Ginsburg, Stevens, and Breyer—in ruling that a punitive forfeiture is forbidden under the Eighth Amendment's excessive fine provision if the forfeiture is "grossly disproportional to the gravity" of the offense. In this case of *United States v. Bajakajian*, an individual successfully challenged the federal government's efforts to keep $357,000 that he had tried to carry out of the country to pay a legal debt in Syria. By law, persons carrying more that $10,000 into or out of the United States are required to declare it. Thomas joined with his more usual lineup of Justices Scalia, Kennedy, O'Connor, and Chief Justice Rehnquist to rule in *Pennsylvania Board of Probation and Parole v. Scott* that illegally seized evidence can be used against defendants in *parole* hearings even if the Fourth Amendment would prevent their use at a *trial*. Justice Thomas's drafting of these two majority opinions, with two such remarkably varied voting blocs, signaled an increase in his ability to cement the crucial five votes needed to decide a case.

Thomas's death penalty jurisprudence is decidedly conservative, with his votes in dissent to uphold the application of capital punishment to mentally retarded murderers (*Atkins v. Virginia* [2002]), to defendants who were juveniles when they committed their offense (*Roper v. Simmons* [2005]), and to child rapists (*Kennedy v. Louisiana* [2008]). He voted with the majority in 2008 to uphold lethal injection (*Baze v. Rees*) as not constituting cruel and unusual punishment and wrote the majority opinion in 2006 to find constitutional a Kansas law under which the death sentence is automatic if the jury finds an equal number of reasons for and against execution (*Kansas v. Marsh*).

Thomas and Scalia were the only dissenters from Chief Justice Rehnquist's 2000 *Dickerson v. U.S.* ruling that validated the Warren Court's liberal interpretation of so-called Miranda Rights, those criminal procedural guarantees that, as of 1966, police must read to suspects. Thomas also sided with government or school authorities in supporting police road blocks with drug-sniffing dogs (dissenting in *Indianapolis v. Edmond* [2000]), as well as random, suspicionless drug testing of student athletes (with the majority in *Vernonia School District v. Acton* [1995]) and student participants in other extra-curricular activities (writing the majority opinion in *Board of Education of Independent School District No. 92 of Pottawatomie City v. Earls* [2002]). He did, however, join his conservative twin, Scalia, in prohibiting, as a violation of privacy, warrantless police use of heat-detecting devices to trace growing of marijuana in private homes (with the majority in *Kyllo v. U.S.*). Thomas supported Scalia's establishment of individual rights to own guns, based on the latter's reading of the Second Amendment, in 2008's *District of Columbia v. Heller*.

Beyond decisions involving the Bill of Rights, one of Thomas's most visible opinions came in the 1995 case *U.S. Term Limits, Inc. v. Thornton*, in which he wrote the lead dissent for Rehnquist, O'Connor, and Scalia. That alignment of four would have upheld the actions of twenty-two states, which by that time had passed laws imposing term limits on their members of Congress. The majority, however, ruled that such limits would violate the uniformity of the federal system; such a major shift in the constitutional order could only be effected through an amendment to the U.S. Constitution. Thomas's dissent harkened back to a pre-Civil War vision of federalism through which the states may act as long as no explicit bar to such actions exists in the Constitution. This theory guided his vote in *Bush v. Gore*, in which he joined Rehnquist's concurrence that Florida must stop recounting votes in the 2000 presidential election because the state's standardless procedures violated both federal guarantees of equal protection and due process.

Justice Thomas, joined only by his steady judicial partner, Justice Scalia, also dissented in two landmark sexual harassment cases that the Court handed down on the last day of its 1997–98 Term. In *Faragher v. City of Boca Raton* and *Burlington Industries, Inc. v. Ellerth*, a seven-person majority developed a rule that employers are vicariously liable if supervisors create a sexually hostile work environment, subject to an affirmative defense by the employer. Justice Thomas's dissent asserted that an employer should be liable for sexual or racial harassment only if the plaintiff proves that the employer was negligent in permitting the supervisor's conduct to occur. In other cases involving gender, Thomas joined the five-person majority in 2007's *Ledbetter v. Goodyear Tire* that narrowed the use of the 1964 Civil Rights Act, Title VII, by women who claimed pay discrimination over the course of their entire careers. Relying on his federalism jurisprudence, Thomas concurred with Rehnquist's voiding of the 1994 Violence Against Women Act in *U.S. v. Morrison* (2000).

Thomas has confirmed the fear that he ascribes to liberal opponents of his nomination over his position on abortion. He has taken every opportunity to limit a woman's right to end her pregnancy, though the pro-life justices (Roberts, Scalia, Thomas, and Alito) have not yet found a fifth vote to overturn *Roe v. Wade*. Justice Kennedy, however, joined them and wrote the majority opinion upholding the federal ban on partial-birth abortions in *Gonzales v. Carhart* (2007). Thomas cannot find an individual right to privacy in the Constitution that would protect homosexual conduct, as the majority did in 2003's *Lawrence v. Texas*. Nevertheless, his dissent noted that, if he were a Texas legislator, he would vote to repeal the state's punishment of "expressing . . . sexual preference through noncommercial consensual conduct with another adult" because it was an "uncommonly silly" law not worthy of expending "valuable law enforcement resources."[18]

Thomas condemns what he calls the "intellectual slavery" that he asserts liberal black interest groups attempt to impose on him.[19] "The Constitution is what matters," he asserts, "not my personal beliefs."[20] He vows to stay on the Court for a long time. Turning sixty in 2008, he is the third youngest member of the Court and could remain on the bench well into the twenty-first century. Despite the controversy that continues to haunt his position on the high tribunal, he has come to view it not just as a job, but as a part of his life itself. Requiring only three or four hours of sleep a night, he rises at 4:00 A.M. each day and tries to arrive at his chambers by 7:00 or 7:30. In 1997 he commented movingly, "For one who thought he lost his vocation when he left the seminary, now I know I did not. This is my vocation."[21] This reassessment of his life's work coincided with his reconversion to Roman Catholicism. Although he and his wife had attended an Episcopal church for many years, he announced at a Holy Cross reunion in 1996 that he had returned to the religion in which his grandparents had raised him. Thomas, who says he "failed" at becoming a priest, now attends daily mass (with his law clerks if they are Catholic). He continues to be inspired by his late grandfather and displays a bust of him in his chambers; the sculpture bears the inscription, "Old Man Can't is dead. I buried him myself." In his 2007 memoir, for which he received a $1.5 million bonus, Thomas described Myers Anderson, the man he called Daddy, as "the one hero in my life. What I am is what he made me."[22]

Justice Thomas may be right about the inevitable failures of those who try to characterize his multilayered life. Critics have indeed portrayed him as a devil, yet among Court employees he is a beloved individual, known for his genuine concern for others and a booming, hearty laugh. He loves cigars and basketball, playing the latter on the "Court's court" until an Achilles tendon injury forced him to the sidelines. A rabid fan of the University of Nebraska (his wife's alma mater) football team, he attends games and team practices when his schedule allows. Thomas also enjoys taking to the highways in either his black Corvette or large recreation vehicle. Sometimes he pulls the latter into Walmart parking lots when he needs a snooze. Attempting to carry on the mentoring legacy of his grandparents, he and his wife took custody of his six-year-old grandnephew (Thomas's sister's grandson) in 1997 and are raising him in their northern Virginia home. Justice Thomas has advised audiences, "You must be able to look yourself in the mirror and like what you see." Only he truly knows the meaning of his own image.

Ruth Bader Ginsburg

"A woman, a mother, a Jew—the kiss of death."[1] With that pithy observation, a friend of Ruth Ginsburg described the very essence of only the second woman ever to serve on the Supreme Court of the United States. As a female, Ginsburg has championed the cause of women's rights both on and off the Court. As a mother, she proudly proclaims the achievements of her children and grandchildren. As a Jew, she has cited "the demand for justice [that] runs through the entirety of the Jewish history and Jewish tradition,"[2] and she has pledged to serve that demand. Yet each characteristic of her essence constituted a professional obstacle, and cumulatively they posed severe handicaps in her early career. That she rose above gender and religious discrimination to achieve such demonstrable success is a tribute to her intellect, perseverance, and character.

Born on March 15, 1933, in Brooklyn, New York, Joan Ruth Bader was the second child of Nathan Bader, who immigrated to the United States at age 12, and Celia Bader, "conceived in the Old World and born in the New World."[3] Ruth's older sister died several years later, and the young girl's parents pinned all their hopes on their surviving daughter. Most girls in the Baders' ethnic neighborhood were expected to marry professional men in order to have a comfortable life, but Ruth's mother taught her to be self-reliant and began saving money for her college tuition. Ginsburg now likes to asks, "What is the difference between a bookkeeper in New York's garment district [her mother's occupation] and a U.S. Supreme Court justice?" The answer: "One generation."[4] "My father spoiled me," Ginsburg remembers. "My mother was the disciplinarian. She told me two things: Be independent and be a lady," which included controlling her emotions.[5]

Nancy Drew, the fictional juvenile sleuth who solves mysteries in a series of books first published in the 1930s, attracted young Ruth's interest: "Here was somebody doing things. She was fearless. She was what every girl would like to be," Ginsburg remembers thinking as a youngster.[6] Ruth Bader's talents and interests emerged early in her education. She graduated first in her class from New York's P.S. 238, where she had written a school newspaper article entitled

"Landmarks of Constitutional Freedom." Appropriately for her interest in constitutional history and her future career path, Ruth attended James Madison High School, named for the "Father of the Constitution." It offered no law-related courses in the future justice's era, but it now has a moot court room named for her. By all accounts, Ruth was a popular, studious, and competitive student there. In addition to receiving stellar grades, especially in English, she enjoyed playing in the school orchestra. Ruth graduated sixth in a senior class from which virtually everyone was college-bound. Sadly, the day before her high school commencement, Ruth's beloved mother—her constant source of inspiration—succumbed to cancer.

Even now, well into her seventies, she seems to call on her youthful strength to bolster those who are grieving a parent's death. In 2005 she wrote a poignant, handwritten note to a scholar who lost her mother just a few days after Justice Ginsburg had offered an introduction to the professor's lecture delivered to Supreme Court Historical Society. "Even when one is all grown up, the death of a parent is a loss like no other. But you have a store of memories to hold dear," she wrote to the 49-year-old scholar. "May you continue to thrive in your work and life, just as your mother would have willed," Justice Ginsburg concluded, capturing the essence of the relationship between a mother and daughter, whom she barely knew.[7]

Although Ruth Bader's mother had carefully saved a nest egg worth $8,000, Ruth gave most of the money to her widowed father and enrolled in Cornell as a scholarship student. At the campus in upstate New York, Bader was a serious student but also enjoyed an active social life beyond the Jewish section of the women's dormitory where the university segregated her and her co-religionists. She met Marty Ginsburg on a blind date during her freshman year and they became fast friends. On Ruth's way to graduating first in her class, one of her favorite courses was constitutional law. When she and Marty Ginsburg decided that their friendship had blossomed into romance and began to make plans for the future, they determined that law would be a professional field they could both share. Marty, one year older than Ruth, enrolled at Harvard Law School. They were married in 1954 at the end of Ruth's undergraduate career, which was capped by her election to Phi Beta Kappa.

After Marty's two-year stint in the Army and the birth of their first child, Jane, in 1955, the Ginsburgs resettled at Harvard Law School—this time with Ruth entering the first-year class as one of only nine women. She compiled a stellar record at Harvard and earned a coveted spot on the law review, despite caring for Jane and nursing Marty through a potentially fatal case of testicular cancer. With Ruth auditing his classes and typing his papers, Marty overcame his illness, graduated on time, and received an offer from a law firm in New York City.

Ruth insisted on keeping the family together and chose to forgo her final year at Harvard. She transferred to Columbia Law School, where she was one of only twelve women in the 353-member class of 1959. At their thirty-fifth reunion, Justice Ginsburg met with her female compatriots and recalled the discrimination they had faced. The women remembered being asked why they were taking a man's place in law school. Justice Ginsburg recollected an incident when a law professor argued that married women were like dogs because men were masters over both. The future justice graduated from Columbia first in her class and earned a spot on another Ivy League law review. Years later she recalled asking Harvard, at the time she was leaving to join Marty in New York, if they might grant her a law degree, even if she completed the third year at Columbia. The school declined, saying that a student had to spend all three years at Harvard in order to receive its degree. The future justice argued that Harvard had awarded a degree to a woman who had transferred in after the first year at another law school, but the Harvard administration would not budge in Ginsburg's case. In 2008 the justice remarked that the current dean of Harvard Law School, a woman, wanted to bestow an honorary degree on Ginsburg, who responded, "No thanks. I've gotten quite a bit of mileage out of the one I have [from Columbia]!"[8]

Despite a superb academic record, like her future colleague Sandra Day O'Connor, Ginsburg found the doors of private law firms closed to her, with not one New York firm offering her a position. Her credentials meant nothing in light of her gender, marital and maternal status, and religious affiliation. She believes that, more so than her religion, the fact that she was a woman and, "the real killer," she adds, the mother of a young child, barred the doors of private practice.[9] Finally, an open-minded U.S. District Court Judge, Edmund L. Palmieri, hired her as his law clerk. Even that good fortune took some arm-twisting by her mentor, Professor Gerald Gunther. Palmieri had expressed his concern that Ginsburg's gender and motherhood might prevent her from working late at night and on weekends, staples of most judicial clerkships. Gunther offered the skeptical judge a "carrot," as Ginsburg puts it: he would substitute a male student if Ginsburg could not live up to her office responsibilities. The corresponding "stick" constituted Gunther's threat that if Palmieri did not hire Ginsburg the professor would never again send him a clerk![10] After her clerkship, Harvard, which was producing a published series on foreign civil law, asked if she would like to accept a research position in Sweden to write the book on that country's legal system because no one else had signed up for the Scandinavian nation. Intrigued by the opportunity to live abroad for several months, and the chance to see her own ideas between the covers of a book, she readily accepted the opportunity.

When Ginsburg returned to the states, Rutgers Law School offered her a teaching position. Her acceptance made her only the second female on the school's faculty and one of the first twenty women law professors in the country. She continued teaching throughout her pregnancy with son James in 1965, hiding her condition under baggy clothes so as not to disrupt her march toward tenure. Shortly thereafter students asked Ginsburg to offer a course on feminist law, and she discovered a dearth of materials on the subject.

Ginsburg could not have imagined that someday she would make such seminal contributions to what is now viewed as the core of landmark gender equity cases. Yet by the early 1970s she knew the legal landscape had to change for women. The final straw for Ginsburg had been the 1961 U.S. Supreme Court decision in Hoyt v. Florida. A battered and abused wife, Mrs. Hoyt, had been convicted by an all-male jury of beating her husband to death with a baseball bat. Florida law included only men in calls for jury duty; women could serve but only if they volunteered for jury service. The Supreme Court's ruling implied that women should feel honored that Florida law recognized the "peculiar characteristics, destiny, and mission of women" that compelled them to be wives and mothers. (And this was from the liberal Warren Court that had so generously interpreted civil rights for blacks.) A vivid metaphor from the pen of a California Supreme Court justice in a 1971 case would resonate with Ginsburg as a counter to the outdated reasoning of the Hoyt decision. The California Court had written: "The pedestal upon which women have been placed has all too often, upon closer inspection, been revealed as a cage."[11]

Ginsburg had the opportunity to borrow the California Court's eloquence and rationale in her capacity as founder and leader of the Women's Rights Law Project of the American Civil Liberties Union in 1971. The U.S. Supreme Court had consistently upheld laws with gender classifications if the government merely could prove a "rational relation" between the classification and the government's legislative goal. Ginsburg developed a brilliant strategy to move the Court gradually away from its previous interpretation of the Fourteenth Amendment's Equal Protection Clause in gender cases. In 1971 she took her first case, Reed v.

Reed, to the Supreme Court, and the future justice has admitted that she did not know if she could keep her breakfast down that morning when she, a petite woman, stepped to the imposing rostrum before the nine men on the highest court in the land. Then she realized that they had to listen to her for the time allotted each side in oral argument, and she overcame a nervous stomach to present her position.

Breaking new ground in gender jurisprudence, the Supreme Court accepted Ginsburg's argument against an Idaho law that required the state to prefer males to females in disputes over who was entitled to administer a will. Viewing such a law as arbitrary and therefore contrary to the Equal Protection Clause, in *Reed* the Supreme Court for the first time held a statute unconstitutional on the grounds that it discriminated against women.

Between 1971 and 1978 Ginsburg argued six precedent-setting cases before the Supreme Court, winning all but one. Most important for women's rights and gender equity in general (Ginsburg brought some of her cases on behalf of *men* who were being denied equal treatment under the law) was that a majority of the justices eventually accepted her argument that gender classifications in laws should be subjected by the courts to a higher level of scrutiny than the rational relation test required. Because of Ginsburg's efforts, the judiciary began to apply a heightened scrutiny to gender classifications and required that the state prove an *important* (not just a rational) relation between the gender distinction and the state interest.

In the meantime, Ginsburg had become the first woman hired with tenure at the Columbia Law School in 1972. (Her daughter Jane eventually accepted a chaired professorship there.) Seven years later President Jimmy Carter, determined to add more women and minorities to the federal judiciary, nominated Ruth Ginsburg for a judgeship on the prestigious U.S. Court of Appeals for the District of Columbia, a traditional training ground for Supreme Court justices. In her thirteen years on that visible bench, she compiled a restrained and moderate, yet distinguished, record.

President Bill Clinton, like his Democratic predecessor Jimmy Carter, vowed to increase the "representativeness" of the federal judiciary by nominating qualified female and minority lawyers to judgeships. Criticism of this policy, however, initially persuaded Clinton to search for a white male when presented with his first opportunity to nominate a member of the Supreme Court following Justice Byron White's retirement announcement in March 1993.[12] Clinton had specified to his advisers that he was also looking for a nominee with a "big heart," presumably to counter the Court's "small-hearted" conservatives. To this end, he announced that he would prefer a politician, rather than a sitting judge, in hopes that such a person would be a natural leader who could encourage the Court's emerging center faction (composed of Justices Sandra O'Connor, Anthony Kennedy, and David Souter) to move further left. Three potential nominees seemed to fit the criterion: New York's Governor Mario Cuomo, Secretary of Education Richard Riley, and Interior Secretary Bruce Babbitt. For a variety of reasons, none of the trio worked out, and Clinton lost hope of finding a politician for the Supreme Court.

Nearly three months had passed since White's announced retirement when Clinton turned to a completely different type of nominee: Stephen Breyer, the chief judge of the U.S. Court of Appeals for the First Circuit in Boston. Breyer, who possessed a superb academic and professional record (including a Supreme Court clerkship for Justice Arthur Goldberg), had the advantage of being relatively moderate and was popular among both Republicans and Democrats in the Senate because of his previous service as counsel to the Senate Judiciary Committee. Yet Breyer had a public relations problem stemming from his failure to pay social security taxes for his part-time cook. Moreover, Breyer, who had just been released from the hospital after a cycling accident, apparently had an awkward luncheon interview with the president. Clinton later told aides that he thought Breyer was selling himself too hard, that his legal interests were too narrow, and that he did not have a "big heart."[13]

As a fallback in case the Breyer nomination did not materialize, Clinton's White House Counsel Bernard Nussbaum had added Ruth Bader Ginsburg to the list of possible nominees. She had first met Bill and Hillary Clinton during the former's governorship of Arkansas. Ginsburg had delivered a lecture at the University of Arkansas–Little Rock, and the governor and first lady had attended. Ruth called husband Marty to say how honored she was that the governor and his wife were in the audience. Ever the comedian, Marty responded, "What else is there to do in Little Rock in the evening!"[14] Regardless of Clinton's motivation for attending Ginsburg's Arkansas talk, she catapulted to the top of the president's list after an hour-and-a-half meeting with him at the White House, during which Clinton "fell in love" with her life's narrative of surviving family tragedies and overcoming personal and professional discrimination.[15]

In announcing her nomination in a Rose Garden ceremony, President Clinton offered three reasons for his selection of Ginsburg: first, her distinguished thirteen-year career on the U.S. Court of Appeals; second, her towering efforts on behalf of women's issues, which made her "to the women's movement what Thurgood Marshall was to the movement for the rights of African Americans"; and third, her proven ability as a consensus builder, as a healer, as a "moderate."[16] Ginsburg's elegant and eloquent acceptance speech, in which she paid tribute to her late mother, moved Clinton to tears, and he excoriated ABC correspondent Brit Hume afterwards when the reporter queried the president about the "zigzag quality" of the selection process that had produced Ginsburg.

Despite Ginsburg's seemingly impeccable feminist credentials, some women's groups did not immediately embrace her nomination. While feminism had evolved in a more radical direction (toward focusing on gender differences), Ginsburg had grown increasingly centrist (still emphasizing gender equality) during her tenure on the circuit court bench. Although supportive of the outcome in *Roe v. Wade*, she had questioned the liberty and privacy rationales of Justice Harry Blackmun's majority opinion in a speech at New York University Law School two months before her nomination. She remained clearly pro-choice (based on her views of equality), but abortion rights advocates, such as Kate Michaelman, president of the National Abortion Rights Action League, commented after Ginsburg's nomination that NARAL would monitor her confirmation hearings carefully to determine whether she "will protect a women's fundamental right to privacy." Despite such doubts, the co-president of the National Women's Law Center, Marcia Greenberger, asserted that "Ruth Ginsburg was as responsible as any one person for legal advances that women made under the Equal Protection Clause of the Constitution. As a result, doors of opportunity have been opened that have benefited not only the women themselves but their families."[17]

The Senate had virtually no doubts about Ginsburg's qualifications for her promotion to the Supreme Court. The Senate Judiciary Committee approved her nomination by a vote of 18–0, and the full Senate followed suit by a 96–3 margin in August 1993. With proud husband Marty Ginsburg holding the Bible, Chief Justice William Rehnquist swore Ruth Bader Ginsburg in as the 107th justice of the Supreme Court in a White House ceremony on August 10, 1993.

Justice Ginsburg's initial terms on the high court demonstrated her normally left-of-center pragmatism that Clinton had described in his Rose Garden nomination. She has voted most frequently with liberal Justices David Souter and John Paul Stevens, and with her pragmatic, centrist colleague Justice Breyer, who in 1994 became Clinton's second nominee to the Supreme Court. Conversely, she infrequently aligns with the conservative wing of the Court, consisting of Chief

Justice John Roberts (his predecessor Chief Justice William Rehnquist) and Justices Antonin Scalia, Clarence Thomas, and Samuel Alito.

In civil rights and liberties cases that address gender, race, or religion, Ginsburg can most often be found on the side of the individual or group claiming a violation of rights. Recalling seeing discriminatory signs ("No dogs or Jews allowed.") at a country inn outside New York City while driving with her parents as a young girl, Ginsburg asserts that "being part of a minority, I know what it is like to be an outsider, what it's like to be the victim of prejudice."[18] Her most visible opinion came in the 1996 VMI decision (*United States v. Virginia*) in which she determined for a 7–1 majority (Thomas having recused himself because his son was a cadet there) that state-funded Virginia Military Institute's exclusion of women from its corps of cadets was unconstitutional. Although Ginsburg's opinion for the Court did not boost gender into the highest category of Fourteenth Amendment equal protection analysis—namely, "suspect classification"—where the state must prove a "compelling" interest in order to treat genders differently, she did argue that the government needs an "exceedingly persuasive justification" for any classification based on sex.

On a statutory matter involving application of the 1964 Civil Rights Act, Title VII, to gender-based pay discrimination, Ginsburg vociferously dissented from Justice Alito's 2007 majority opinion strictly applying the 180-day window (after the initial discriminatory act) for women to bring suit against employers. Exercising a rarely used prerogative, Ginsburg read her dissent from the bench. She observed that women often do not know how much their male counterparts are earning and that the discrimination may be cumulative over a period of years, rather than in one paycheck. Ginsburg called on Congress to amend Title VII to remove the 180-day limit. Senator Hillary Clinton (D.-N.Y.) led the effort, which ultimately fell short.

Ginsburg has provided predictable votes for access to abortion. In *Stenberg v. Carhart* (2000) and *Gonzales v. Carhart* (2007), she sided, first with the majority, and, then with the dissents, to strike down state and federal bans on partial-birth procedures. Her lead dissent in *Gonzales*, which she also read from the bench, expressed staunch opposition to bans on late-term abortions that took no consideration of mothers' health concerns. She was particularly outraged at the Court's argument, via Justice Anthony Kennedy's majority opinion, that women must be protected from the consequences of allegedly seeking abortions without understanding their impact. Ginsburg cited a litany of decisions, beginning in the nineteenth century, that purported to protect women based on the Court's view of their physical and mental weaknesses. Of course, Ginsburg had litigated successfully against such outmoded generalizations as head of the ACLU's Women's Rights Law Project in the 1970s. She also cast her vote, in dissent, to uphold the 1994 Violence Against Women Act (*U.S. v. Morrison*).

In the three important race cases of the 1994–95 term that signaled the Supreme Court's retreat from past precedents favoring minorities, Justice Ginsburg dissented. She questioned the majority's holding in *Adarand v. Peña*, which required that federal affirmative action plans pass the highest level of equal protection analysis; took issue with the Court's opinion in *Miller v. Johnson*, which banned the use of race as the predominant criterion in drawing congressional district boundaries; and departed from the majority opinion in *Missouri v. Jenkins II*, which overturned lower court decrees ordering massive expenditures to create integrated magnet schools.

Ginsburg happily joined the majority, led by Justice Sandra Day O'Connor in 2003's *Grutter v. Bollinger*, upholding the University of Michigan Law School's affirmative action policy of using race as a "plus" when considering admission of "underrepresented minorities," namely, African Americans, Hispanics, and Native Americans. She filed a brief concurrence with O'Connor's belief that such policies would no longer be necessary in twenty-five years. Ginsburg cited international treaties to support her position, which raised a firestorm in Congress and among conservative talk-radio hosts who lambasted her use of "foreign" legal authority, despite the fact that the treaties were ratified by the United States. After producing statistics to indicate the continuing racial separation and bias in America, she concluded, "From today's vantage point, one may hope, but not firmly forecast, that over the next generation's span, progress toward nondiscrimination and genuine equal opportunity will make it safe to sunset affirmative action."[19] Her stance forced Ginsburg into the minority in the companion case of *Gratz v. Bollinger*, where the Court voided the University of Michigan undergraduate college's assignment of bonus points to minority applicants.

Whereas Ginsburg willingly applies equal protection analysis to benefit women and minorities, she had no desire to use it as the conservative majority did to stop the recount of votes in Florida after the deadlocked 2000 presidential election. She and Justice Stevens wrote stinging dissents in *Bush v. Gore*. Hers ended with the terse, "I dissent," instead of the more traditional and diplomatic, "I respectfully dissent." The media made much over the distinction, but she did not rise to the bait. In fact, many years later she tells audiences that Justice Scalia, who was on the other side in the historic decision, called her chambers as the ruling in Bush's favor was about to be announced late at night in mid-December. He inquired about how she was doing and encouraged her to go home and take a hot bath!

In church and state cases, Justice Ginsburg has hewed to the separationist line preferred by liberals. She joined the Court's five-person majority in the 1994 case of *Board of Education of Kiryas Joel Village v. Grumet* when it held that New York state may not carve out a separate school district to accommodate the special needs of a particular community of "highly religious Satmar Hasidic Jews." In two 1995 cases she dissented from majority rulings that represented to her impermissible mixing of government and religion. They were *Rosenberger v. University of Virginia*, requiring the university to subsidize a student-run Christian magazine through funds collected from the student activities fee, and *Capitol Square Review Board v. Pinette*, upholding the Ku Klux Klan's erection of a cross on the state capitol grounds in Columbus, Ohio. In addition, she was among the dissenters in the 1997 case *Agostini v. Felton*, which held that public school teachers may now provide remedial instruction for children *inside* parochial schools under Title I of the Federal Aid to Elementary and Secondary Schools Act of 1965. Her dissenting opinion, however, avoided the broad constitutional arguments of her fellow dissenters and focused on the procedural issues of the case.[20] On the issue of school prayer, which the Court addressed in *Santa Fe School Independent School District v. Doe* (2000), she voted with the six-justice majority to prohibit student-led prayers over the public-address system at Texas high school football games. In *Zelman v. Simmons-Harris* (2002), Ginsburg joined an angry dissent by Justice Souter in which he accused the majority's sanction of government vouchers for students to attend private schools, including religiously affiliated ones, as fomenting divisiveness among denominations. She voted in 2003's Ten Commandment cases (*McCreary County v. American Civil Liberties Union* and *Van Orden v. Perry*) to prohibit government display in courthouses and presentation on state capitol grounds, respectively, of the Decalogue.

In a variety of criminal rights controversies, Ginsburg has sliced through the complex verbiage of federal and state statutes with the skill and precision of a surgeon. Her 1997 opinion for a nearly unanimous Court in *Chandler v. Miller* struck down a Georgia statute requiring candidates for designated state offices to certify that they had taken a urinalysis drug test, with a negative result, within thirty days prior to qualifying for nomination or election. Searching in vain for explicit proof of Georgia's "special need" to overcome Fourth Amendment guarantees against unreasonable search and seizure, Justice Ginsburg declared the state law unconstitutional. Again relying on her commitment to Fourth Amendment rights, she authored the minority's dissenting opinion in *Board of Education of Independent School District No. 92 of Pottawatomie County v. Earls* (2002). The five-justice majority upheld the district's mandatory random drug testing for students participating in extracurricular activities. Ginsburg declared the policy unconstitutional as an unreasonable search. She joined with five other colleagues to support Justice Kennedy's 2003 majority opinion invalidating Texas's prohibition of "homosexual conduct." Her broad view of privacy led her to support the personal autonomy of consenting adults to choose sexual practices common among same-sex partners.

In 1998 Ginsburg constructed a heated dissent, joined by the unusual alignment of Chief Justice Rehnquist and Justices Scalia and Souter, from the Breyer-authored majority ruling in *Muscarello v. United States*. The Court ruled that Congress's statutory language "uses or carries a firearm" "during and in relation to" a "drug trafficking crime" encompassed a handgun locked in the glove compartment of Muscarello's car, which he used to transport marijuana for sale. Ginsburg, pointedly arguing that unlike the majority she did not have to rely on dictionaries for statutory meaning, urged a narrow definition of "carry" (bear in "such a manner as to be ready for use as a weapon") that could logically be gleaned from the relevant context of the statute. On the more straightforward issue of gun control, she dissented from the Court's 2008 *District of Columbia v. Heller* ruling that struck down Washington's ban on handguns as violative of the Second Amendment's right to individual gun ownership.

Although each of these cases garnered headlines, and several will be deemed landmarks long into the future, Justice Ginsburg's reasoning in her opinions has proved much less sweeping than that of paradigmatic liberals like Justices William J. Brennan, Jr., and Thurgood Marshall or Chief Justice Earl Warren, who preceded her on the bench. Her *VMI* decision is illustrative; instead of boosting gender into the "suspect category," requiring a compelling interest from the state in order to classify on the basis of sex, Ginsburg argued that a state must demonstrate an "exceedingly persuasive justification" for using gender-based distinctions. Did she split the difference between "heightened scrutiny" and "strict scrutiny"? Commentators are divided on how to interpret her language, but it is certain that a more activist judge in the Brennan mold would have taken the opportunity to rule broadly by placing gender on a par with race in equal-protection analysis. Moreover, as symbolically meaningful as the *VMI* ruling was, it was substantively applicable only to two schools: the state-run, all-male military academies of Virginia Military Institute and the Citadel. After the decision came down, the media were anxious to speculate on how the opinion would apply to single-gender private colleges or primary and secondary public school programs that are segregated by gender. Yet the Ginsburg opinion gave no hint of how the Court would rule on those different situations. As Ginsburg has commented generally on her approach to drafting rulings for the Court: "I continue to aim for opinions that both get it right, and keep it tight, without undue digressions or decorations or distracting denunciations of colleagues who hold different views."[21]

So in both jurisprudence and personality, Justice Ginsburg is somewhat of a paradox: a pioneer in the feminist revolution of the 1970s but a jurist wedded to the incrementalism of the rule of law; a quiet, reserved, diminutive fixture at the Court's public receptions but a willing, delighted "extra" in period costume on the stage of the Washington Opera; a moderate liberal whose close friend on the Court is archconservative Antonin Scalia because, Ginsburg reports, he makes her laugh. (Scalia, also an opera buff, appeared with her in powdered wig and knee breeches in the production of Richard Strauss's *Ariadne auf Naxos*. A photograph of the two of them together on stage is one of Justice Ginsburg's favorites.) They and their spouses spend every New Year's Eve together.

Ginsburg's demure and deliberate social persona vanishes on the bench, where she is a frequent, incisive, and insistent questioner during oral arguments. Shortly after she arrived at the high court, stories appeared in the media that Justice O'Connor was annoyed that her questions were being interrupted by Ginsburg. When asked about the alleged conflict, Justice Ginsburg explained that she could not always see her colleagues, or determine when they were speaking, from the far end of the bench where by tradition the most junior justice sits. More to the point, she related her amusement that the press never reports male justices interrupting other male justices (which happens quite frequently on this very vocal Court). Justice Ginsburg, however, prefers to accentuate the positive experiences of serving on the Supreme Court, reporting that in private the justices have "heated discussions, lively discussions, but not what one would regard as angry disagreements. This place specializes in reason. We reason together."[22]

Since Justice O'Connor retired, leaving the Court in 2006 to be replaced by Justice Samuel Alito, Ginsburg repeatedly tells audiences at every opportunity that it is wrong to have only one woman among the nine members of the highest court in the land. Looking back on her unprecedented career, Ginsburg responds bemusedly when asked if it has gone as she planned. With the limited opportunities available to her generation, she literally could not have planned her professional trajectory. Justice Ginsburg observes that she and Sandra Day O'Connor were simply in the right place at the right time. If they were men, she comments with a wry smile, they both would now be retired senior partners at major law firms! Despite year-long chemotherapy treatment for colorectal cancer nearly a decade ago, Justice Ginsburg, a diminutive, petite woman, shows no signs of retiring, even in her mid-seventies. The talent, determination, diligence, and familial support that initially brought her to the "Marble Palace" will help her to counter the aging process as long as she can—or perhaps until a Democratic president promises to replace her with another woman.

CHAPTER EIGHT

Stephen G. Breyer

Shortly after his elevation to the Supreme Court of the United States, Justice Breyer was flying to San Francisco, his birthplace, to speak at a Stanford University alumni event. In the seat next to him was a San Francisco attorney who asked Breyer what he did for a living. The new justice responded modestly that he was "a judge." When the lawyer asked on what court, Breyer stated vaguely "the Supreme Court." And when the persistent passenger questioned at which level, Breyer had to reveal his status and say, "United States." To which the attorney exclaimed, "Oh, you must be Shirley Black's nephew!" referring to Breyer's aunt, who was a well-known labor lawyer in the City by the Bay.[1] The anecdote illustrates the relative anonymity in which members of the U.S. Supreme Court labor. Nevertheless, prior to his promotion to the nation's highest court, Stephen Breyer was well known among his judicial colleagues as a "judge's judge." As a longtime friend put it, "Stephen Breyer is not only the best judge in the United States, but everybody knows it."[2] His Aunt Shirley had always known he would be "something great" because baby Stephen "started speaking in complete sentences."[3]

Breyer's background aptly predicted his success. His father, Irving, was a lawyer and counsel to the San Francisco Board of Education for forty-two years. His mother, Anne, was active in public affairs through the local Democratic Party and the League of Women Voters. Both parents encouraged young Stephen, born August 15, 1938, and his younger brother Charles to participate in the real world as well as the world of ideas. Mr. Breyer enjoyed entertaining his family with colorful stories of the conflicts between political factions in the public education arena, and Mrs. Breyer's membership in the United Nations Association ensured that an array of international figures streamed through the Breyer household. As was typical of the large middle-class Jewish community in San Francisco, the Breyers put a premium on formal education. Stephen attended a public elementary school and Lowell High School, an academically rigorous public institution, where he excelled, seemingly effortlessly. He won prizes for his performances in math and science, as well as for his debating skills. Prophetically, he was voted "most likely to succeed." True to form, he also achieved the rank of Eagle Scout as a member of the Boy Scouts, though on outings he earned the dubious moniker, "Blister King."

Stephen narrowed his college choices to Harvard and Stanford, and his mother, worried that her elder son would become too isolated and scholarly if he chose Harvard, urged him to select Stanford for its well-rounded approach to education. Like his father, and eventually his own son, Breyer chose to pursue his undergraduate degree at Stanford. His grades there were perfect except for one B (which left him "distraught," in the words of a classmate), and he graduated in 1959 with "Great Distinction" and a Phi Beta Kappa membership. His lack of athletic prowess doomed his attempt to earn a Rhodes Scholarship, but he fulfilled his desire to attend Oxford University by winning a Marshall Scholarship. At Oxford's Magdalen College, he successfully pursued friendships with the British students (no easy feat for an American), and achieved the equally difficult goal of earning a "First Class" ranking for his 1961 degree in politics, philosophy, and economics.

Despite eschewing Harvard for his undergraduate studies, Breyer returned from England to enroll at Harvard Law School. He thrived on the rigorous Socratic method used by Harvard's elite professors to intimidate first-year law students. While most of the students dreaded the thought of being called upon and slouched in their seats to avoid being recognized, Breyer eagerly volunteered to respond to the professors' questions. One classmate from that era remembers thinking about Breyer's intellect and willingness to debate, "This guy will be heard from again."[4]

Some of his research at Harvard concentrated on pragmatism and the law, with Breyer theorizing that judges should determine the social, political, and legal impact of their decisions on the people affected by their outcomes. Once more, Breyer compiled a first-rate record; he was elected to the *Harvard Law Review*, where he served as articles editor, and graduated *magna cum laude* in 1964. Recognizing his stellar performance, Supreme Court Justice Arthur Goldberg invited Breyer to be his law clerk for one year after leaving Harvard Law School. During Breyer's tenure as a clerk in 1964–65, the Supreme Court handed down its landmark decision in *Griswold v. Connecticut*, which invalidated a state law prohibiting the distribution of contraceptives to married couples. The majority opinion, written by Justice William O. Douglas, extrapolated a right to privacy from the "penumbras" and "emanations" of the Bill of Rights, including its Ninth

Amendment, which states that "the enumeration in the Constitution, of certain rights, shall not be construed to deny or disparage others retained by the people."[5] Justice Goldberg contributed a concurring opinion, drafted by Breyer, expounding on the Ninth Amendment's foundation for discovering rights not explicitly guaranteed in the Constitution.

After his clerkship, Breyer remained in Washington as a special assistant to the assistant attorney general in the Department of Justice's Antitrust Division. During this two-year stint in the nation's capital, he met Joanna Hare, a twenty-four-year-old assistant to the *London Sunday Times* Washington correspondent, at a Georgetown dinner party in 1966. Joanna, the daughter of Lord Blakenham, who once led Britain's Conservative Party and was heir to a British media fortune, had an Oxford degree in politics, philosophy, and economics; Breyer had also studied "PPE" on his Marshall Scholarship to Oxford. In addition, the couple shared a love of bicycling and camping. She admired his wit and intelligence; he enjoyed her lovely demeanor and sharp intellect that challenged his own. In September 1967 they married at a village church in Suffolk, England. Because Breyer is Jewish, references to Christ were expunged from the Church of England wedding ceremony.

The newlyweds settled in Cambridge, Massachusetts, where Stephen accepted an assistant professorship at Harvard Law School and Joanna earned a master's degree in education and a doctorate in psychology from Harvard. She gave birth to three children (Chloe in 1969, Nell in 1971, and Michael in 1974) and eventually became a clinical psychologist at the Dana Farber Cancer Institute in Boston, specializing in juvenile leukemia cases.[6]

Stephen Breyer carved out a niche teaching and researching antitrust issues, administrative law, and economic regulation, and he was promoted to full professor at Harvard in 1970, a position he held for a decade, with several return engagements in Washington for government service. Indeed, his parents would have been proud of his combining the scholarly life with contributions to public affairs. In 1973 Breyer served as an assistant special prosecutor for the Watergate Special Prosecution Force, and in 1974–75 he was special counsel to the Administrative Practices Subcommittee of the U.S. Senate Judiciary Committee. He returned in 1979–80 as the Judiciary Committee's chief counsel. In the last position, he exhibited his skill in bipartisan negotiating, especially in his work on deregulation of the airline industry, which allowed him to embody his pragmatic approach to law and economics. Breyer believes that laws can strike a balance between the free market and government regulation necessary to protect consumers. Thus, business and industry are free to be productive and profitable, but not at the expense of and injury to the American people. Airline deregulation produced decidedly mixed results, including lower airfares and bankruptcies of unprofitable carriers. Nevertheless, the policy showcased Breyer's prodigious intellectual and political talents.

The latter stood him in good stead when President Jimmy Carter nominated him for a seat on the U.S. Court of Appeals for the First Circuit at the end of his term in 1980. The change of parties in both the White House and Senate doomed other last-minute Carter nominees, but Breyer received support from Republicans as well as Democrats, ensuring his confirmation. Once on the Court of Appeals, Breyer again displayed his legal pragmatism. His opinions, which he insisted on writing himself without using footnotes (after Justice Goldberg suggested that he drop citations), were noted for their brevity, incisiveness, and ability to persuade the two other members of the typical three-judge panel. Strict adherence to the facts of a case, rather than sweeping conclusions, was the hallmark of Breyer's appellate opinions. In 1985 he began a four-year term on the U.S. Sentencing Commission, where he put his technical expertise to work in overhauling federal criminal sentencing guidelines for judges. He developed a complex grid or template into which judges had to plug factors such as the severity of a crime and the defendant's past criminal record. Proponents of the system argued that it standardized a previously idiosyncratic system, but federal judges complained about the loss of discretion in sentencing decisions. Civil libertarians maintained that it put a premium on law and order while discriminating against first-time offenders and black males. In a 1989 case, *Mistretta v. United States*, the U.S. Supreme Court upheld the constitutionality of the U.S. Sentencing Commission. Breyer's obvious administrative and consensus-building talents vaulted him into the chief justiceship of the First Circuit in 1990; in that position he planned a stunning new federal courthouse overlooking Boston Harbor. It has earned both kudos and criticism for its opulence.

Not surprisingly, Breyer's judicial record on the Court of Appeals was considered moderately liberal and marked by a continuing interest in antitrust cases, in which he attempted to find the happy medium between business concerns and the public good. His centrist posture dovetailed perfectly with Bill Clinton's own ideology, and the new president seriously considered Breyer for the Supreme Court seat vacated by Justice Byron White's retirement in the spring of 1993. After an unsuccessful attempt at finding a politician with a "big heart" for his first Supreme Court nomination, Clinton turned to Breyer. Leaving his hospital bed, to which he was confined with a punctured lung and broken ribs after a cycling accident, Breyer took the train to Washington, where he was met at Union Station by the ill-fated Associate White House Counsel Vincent Foster (who would commit suicide a few weeks later). Breyer's impeccable credentials could not overcome an awkward luncheon conversation between Clinton and the ailing judge or the fact that he and his wife had neglected to pay social security taxes for their part-time cook. Such an issue had derailed President Clinton's first nominee for attorney general, Zoe Baird. The president then turned to Judge Ruth Bader Ginsburg of the U.S. Court of Appeals for the District of Columbia, whose nomination to the Supreme Court sailed smoothly through the Senate.

Instead of sulking over his bad luck, Breyer graciously attended Ginsburg's swearing-in ceremony—a cordial gesture not lost on President Clinton. When Justice Harry Blackmun announced his retirement from the Supreme Court the next year, Breyer's name went back on the list of candidates who might succeed him. Clinton still longed to place a politician in the Earl Warren mold on the high court, but Senate Majority Leader George Mitchell, an erstwhile federal judge, declined. Nominating Interior Secretary Bruce Babbitt, the former governor of Arizona, threatened to provoke a Senate battle, which Clinton could ill afford while his proposed health care reform bill siphoned off his meager political capital. Clinton leaned toward his longtime Arkansas friend Judge Richard Arnold of the U.S. Court of Appeals for the Eighth Circuit but eventually jettisoned his nomination, fearing charges of cronyism and controversy over Arnold's previous bout with cancer.

Breyer's former boss at the Senate Judiciary Committee, Senator Edward Kennedy (D.-Mass.), lobbied hard for the jurist from his home state. Again attracting bipartisan support, as he had for his initial nomination to the federal bench, Breyer won praise from Senator Orrin Hatch (R.-Utah), who urged President Clinton to nominate him. Noting Breyer's backing from two such diverse partisans, the president did so on May 13, 1994. Although he had debated several weeks over Blackmun's replacement, Clinton was so quick with his announcement once the decision to nominate Breyer was made that the appeals court judge could not travel from Boston to Washington quickly enough to be at the president's side. Instead, a formal appearance for Clinton and Breyer in the White House Rose Garden took place several days after the initial nomination. In offering Breyer's name to the Senate and the American people, the president emphasized that the appellate jurist possessed "a clear grasp of the law, a boundless respect for the constitutional and legal rights of the American people, a searching and restless intellect and a remarkable ability to explain complex subjects in understandable terms."[7] Responding to his selection, Breyer vowed to interpret the law to benefit ordinary people and echoed the American people's faith in the Supreme Court. With his exemplary academic and professional record (he had served in all three branches of government) and his talent for forging consensus, Breyer earned unanimous approval from the Senate Judiciary Committee. He then garnered confirmation from the full Senate by a vote of 87–9 on July 29, 1994, with the opposition led by Richard Lugar (R.-Ind.), who questioned the propriety of several investment ventures Breyer had made, particularly one with Lloyds of London.

The newly confirmed justice would experience three separate swearing-in ceremonies. The first occurred at Chief Justice William Rehnquist's summer home in Vermont on August 3, 1994, so that Breyer could begin to start work and hire his law clerks. Eight days later a more formal ceremony took place at the White House, followed by the Court's public investiture of Breyer just before the opening of its 1994–95 term in October. Justice Breyer immediately distinguished himself as a frequent and professorial questioner at oral argument. Unfailingly polite to counsel in the unenviable position of debating complex questions before the Supreme Court, Breyer often poses multipart queries in a classroom lecture style. Sometimes he pitches his body forward on the bench, leaning on his elbows and cradling his bald head in his hands, as he earnestly attempts to decipher a counsel's response. He and Justice Clarence Thomas, who sits next to him, often rock back in their chairs and chat amiably.

Breyer throws himself into his job with a youthful zeal that belies his seventy years of age. In an interview conducted eight months after he assumed his position on the Supreme Court, he remarked about his new job, "I am very enthusiastic about it. I might find myself here fairly late in the evenings, simply because time is passing quickly and I am finding what I am doing so fascinating."[8] In January 1995 he became so excited in summarizing his first opinion for the Court, in a case that arose out of an extermination company's termite contract, that he forgot to add that there were two dissenting opinions. After he concluded his scholarly synopsis and remained silent, Justice Thomas and then-Chief Justice William Rehnquist both stage-whispered, "The dissents!" A bit sheepishly, Breyer smiled and replied, "Oh, there was a dissent [actually two] as well."

Justice Breyer occasionally adds a touch of impish wit to the oral argument. In April 1995 the Court heard the case of *Vernonia School District v. Acton*, which raised the question of whether random drug testing (through urinalysis) of middle- and high-school student athletes who have not engaged in suspicious behavior is constitutional. Chief Justice Rehnquist opened the way for some "locker room humor" with his reasoning that urinalysis is hardly a violation of privacy when boys' locker rooms are rarely private, with their rows of open urinals and "guys walking around naked." Justice Breyer added that he did not think that providing a urine sample was necessarily an intrusion on privacy because urination is a fact of life. Or as the new justice put it (betraying a male perspective), "It isn't really a tremendously private thing." For the record, the attorney for Vernonia student James Acton had to concede that everyone urinates. The lawyer, visibly nervous over this line of questioning on a rather delicate subject, added, "In fact, I might do so here!" With that frank admission-cum-quip, which brought a spontaneous eruption of laughter from the audience, he bested Rehnquist and Breyer with some improvised humor of his own. Ultimately, the Court ruled against Acton and in favor of the Vernonia School District's drug-testing policy; Justice Breyer joined the majority in the 6–3 decision. He would do so again when the Court upheld a similar policy for students in all extracurricular activities (*Board of Education of Independent School District No. 92 of Pottawatomie County v. Earls* [2002]),

Yet despite occasional humorous exchanges on the bench, Breyer performs his role on the Supreme Court with the utmost respect for the institution he serves. In June 1995, just eight months after he was sworn in as the 108th justice of the Supreme Court, Breyer presided over the swearing-in ceremony for the new directors of the Holocaust Museum in Washington, D.C. The seventh Jewish member to serve on the high court in its history, Breyer was an obvious choice to read the oath of office for each new director. Standing in the museum's Hall of Remembrance with its eternal flame flickering in the background, Breyer began with a remembrance of his first tour through the museum. Like many others who have taken the several-hour journey through the barbarism that marked the Holocaust, he had been overcome with emotion and rendered speechless after the experience. In addition to an emotional reaction based on his own Jewish background, he was also overcome by thoughts related to his status as a lawyer and a judge. He recalled that there were laws, lawyers, and judges in Nazi Germany, but they had not prevented—indeed they had sometimes facilitated—the terror and annihilation that marked the horrific reign of Hitler's Third Reich. He noted that Americans often express frustration over the inefficiency of the United States government, but Breyer reminded his audience that their frustration results from the separation of powers, which the Founders designed to curb the kind of unrestrained power that German Nazis exercised.

Justice Breyer then spoke of his new job at the Supreme Court in a voice filled with passion and awe. He observed, "I go into this courtroom . . . and I feel this history. This is the room in which *Brown v. Board of Education* was decided. This is the room in which so many things of historic importance have transpired. And the feeling that I get is a feeling of responsibility. I must take part in an institution that has to transmit from the past these traditions and values to the next generation."[9]

Breyer has also spoken movingly of the need to continue the fight against racial, religious, and gender discrimination, noting that his own father was barred from social clubs at Stanford because he was Jewish. Not surprisingly, on the Supreme Court Breyer has championed civil rights and liberties generally (with some notable exceptions in the criminal rights realm), almost always joining the Stevens-Souter-Ginsburg group on such issues. In his first two terms on the high bench, Breyer most frequently sided with Ginsburg and least frequently with Thomas and Scalia. He voted with the dissenters in the 1995 affirmative action case *Adarand v. Peña*, which required federal government preferences for minority businesses to meet the highest level of scrutiny, and he also aligned with the minority in the racial gerrymandering cases of 1995 that struck down congressional districts drawn with race as the predominant consideration.

Breyer sided with the majority in the 2003 landmark University of Michigan Law School ruling (*Grutter v. Bollinger*), where Justice Sandra Day O'Connor validated the use of race as a "plus" in admissions decisions. Two years later Justice Breyer published a slim volume, *Active Liberty: Interpreting Our Democratic Constitution*, based on a series of lectures he delivered at Harvard in late 2004. He defined "active liberty" as the nation's sharing of its sovereign authority with its citizens. Interpretation of the Constitution, he maintained, should consider not only those tenets known as "originalism," that is, text, history, tradition, and precedent, but also the purpose of the text, its language and values, and the consequences of judicial decisions. He explained that Justice O'Connor's majority opinion in *Grutter*, with which he agreed, reflected the principles of active liberty, as he defined them. These principles, Breyer declared, "find some form of affirmative action necessary to maintain a well-functioning participatory democracy. . . . [Without affirmative action] [t]oo many individuals of all races would lack experience with a racially diverse educational environment helpful for their later effective participation in today's diverse society. Too many individuals of the minority race would find the doors of higher education closed; those closed doors would shut them out of positions of leadership in the armed forces, in business, and in government as well. . . . If these are the likely consequences—as many knowledgeable groups told the Court they were—could our democratic form of government then function as the Framers intended?"[10] Nevertheless, Breyer concurred with the judgment of the *Gratz v. Bollinger* conservative majority invalidating the UM undergraduate college's use of a 20-point bonus for minorities in admissions.

The voluntary use of race and ethnicity by public schools in Seattle and Louisville to make assignments of students to schools in order to diversify them provoked a passionate response from Justice Breyer. A five-person majority struck down the policies as violative of the Fourteen Amendment's Equal Protection Clause. Breyer authored the lead dissent and spent nearly thirty minutes reading it word for word from the bench on the very last day of the Court's 2006–07 term. He fervently believed that the plans to prevent resegregation of public schools were constitutional, as were their goals of racial unity, rather than division. He lambasted the five majority votes that thwarted these goals, declaring, "It is not often in the law that so few have so quickly changed so much," and he predicted that their decision was one "the court and nation will come to regret."[11]

In religion cases Justice Breyer voted on the separationist side (each time in dissent) in the 1995 *Rosenberger* case requiring the University of Virginia to provide funds from the student-activities fee to a student-sponsored Christian magazine, and in the 1997 New York decision allowing public school remedial instructors to teach in parochial schools (*Agostini v. Felton*). He sided with the accommodationists, however, in the Columbus, Ohio, Ku Klux Klan case, sanctioning that city's public forum, which is open to a variety of private expression, both religious (in this instance a cross erected by the Klan) and nonreligious (*Capitol Square Review Board v. Pinette*). Justice Breyer returned to the separationist fold in voting with the 2000 majority to void student-led prayers sanctioned by Texas public schools at football games (*Santa Fe Independent School District v. Doe*) and with the dissenters in the 2002 ruling upholding government-sponsored vouchers with which parents could send their children to private, including parochial, schools (*Zelman v. Simmons-Harris*). He arrived at a split result, however, in the 2005 Ten Commandment cases, providing the swing votes that prohibted Kentucky counties from displaying copies of the Decalogue in their courthouses (*McCreary County v. American Civil Liberties Union*) but allowed Texas to keep a granite display of the commandments, donated over forty years previously by a civic organization, on its capitol grounds (*Van Orden v. Perry*).

Under the First Amendment's Free Exercise Clause, Breyer voted (in dissent) to uphold the Religious Freedom Restoration Act as a valid exercise of Congress's authority to require the highest level of protection for religious claims against government regulation (*City of Boerne v. Flores* [1997]).

On free expression issues Breyer has compiled a mixed record. In *Denver Area Educational Telecommunications Consortium, Inc. v. Federal Communications Commission* (1996), Justice Breyer upheld First Amendment claims by challengers of regulatory statutes applying to cable television. Television viewers in the Denver case had challenged portions of the Cable Television Consumer Protection and Competition Act of 1992, as implemented by the FCC. Breyer's opinion for the Court struck down the Act's provision that required operators of leased access channels to segregate "patently offensive" programming on a single channel, to block that channel from viewer access, and to unblock it (or later reblock it) within thirty days of a subscriber's written request. Breyer reasoned that such a requirement was overly restrictive and its benefits speculative. Eight years later, however, he sided in favor of the government's Child Online Protection Act, writing a dissent from the majority's ruling that the law shielding children from Internet pornography swept too broadly in its content restrictions. His support of Congress's effort to fight child pornography on the Web by criminalizing "pandering" of real or purported obscene materials added to the 7–2 victory in *U.S. v. Williams* (2008).

In campaign finance, Justice Breyer upheld the right of the Federal Campaign Committee (Colorado Party) to fund, independently of any GOP candidate, radio advertisements attacking the Democratic Party's likely candidate. Dollar limits imposed by the Federal Election Campaign Act of 1971 on such activities were an unconstitutional violation of the First Amendment, argued Breyer in his opinion for the Court (*Colorado Republican Federal Campaign Committee v. Federal Election Commission* [1996]). He was among the five-justice majority that found no First Amendment violations in the McCain-Feingold Bipartisan Campaign Reform Act's limits on "soft money" contributions and advertising (*McConnell v. Federal Election Commission* [2004]). But he wrote the majority opinion striking down Vermont's caps (the lowest in the nation) on campaign contributions and candidate spending as unconstitutional limits on free speech (*Randall v. Sorrell* [2006]).

The issue of student speech rights faced the Court in 2007's *Morse v. Frederick,* which presented the question of whether public schools may punish student speech displayed at a school-sanctioned and school-supervised event. A senior at a Juneau, Alaska, public high school, Frederick held up a banner with the words "Bong Hits 4 Jesus" across the street from the school during a parade in honor of the Olympic torch-bearer, which students had permission to attend. The Court supported the school, arguing that it had the authority to enforce the district's anti-drug policy. Justice Breyer concurred in part and dissented in part, agreeing that the Court's decision was "unlikely to undermine First Amendment principles," but declaring that resolving the question in this case was "unwise and unnecessary."[12] Breyer foresaw an influx of student speech cases requiring federal courts throughout the land to settle school disciplinary disputes.

Justice Breyer produced a noteworthy dissent in the 1995 landmark *U.S. v. Lopez* case, in which the 5–4 majority invalidated the Gun-Free School Zones Act of 1990 on the grounds that it had exceeded Congress's authority to regulate interstate commerce. Applying his economic reasoning to the dispute, Breyer argued that, if Congress found that guns disrupted schools to such an extent as to affect education's impact on interstate and foreign commerce, the legislature was well within its constitutional purview to implement a gun-free school zone policy. Likewise, Breyer voted with the dissenters in *U.S. v. Morrison* (2000) who would have upheld the Violence Against Women Act as a valid exercise of the Congress's interstate commerce power. After *Lopez,* Congress gathered mountains of data to prove that violence against females had an impact on business and commerce. Breyer also dissented in the 1997 Brady Act case, which invalidated the portion of the *national* gun control act that required *state* law-enforcement authorities to maintain records of gun purchases. Whereas the Court's majority found the statute's requirement to be a violation of federalism, Breyer argued in his dissent that "there is no need to interpret the Constitution as containing an absolute principle—forbidding the assignment of virtually any federal duty to any state officer."[13] Additionally, he dissented from 2008's landmark *District of Columbia v. Heller* ruling nullifying Washington's hand-gun ban as a violation of the Second Amendment.

In death penalty litigation, Breyer voted with the majorities that struck down capital punishment for mentally retarded defendants (*Atkins v. Virginia* [2002]) and for juvenile offenders (*Roper v. Simmons* [2005]). Likewise, he voted to ban the death penalty for child rapists (*Kennedy v. Louisiana* [2008]). He could not, however, find a violation of the Eighth Amendment's guarantee against cruel and unusual punishment in the challenged three-drug protocol used by states and the federal government to administer lethal injections (*Baze v. Rees* [2008]).

In two major abortion cases involving state (*Stenberg v. Carhart* [2000]) and federal (*Gonzales v. Carhart* [2007]) bans on partial-birth procedures, Justice Breyer voted to void the prohibitions. His position placed him with the majority in *Stenberg*, where he authored the opinion of the Court, arguing that the state ban in Nebraska placed an "undue burden" on women and provided no health exceptions for mothers. He dissented in *Gonzales*, when the majority upheld the federal ban on late-term abortions. In 2003's *Lawrence v. Texas* Justice Breyer joined the majority to nullify state prohibitions of homosexual acts, ruling that rights to personal privacy protected such behavior between consenting adults.

Regarding presidential immunity, Breyer's concurrence in *Clinton v. Jones*, which almost read like a dissent, was prescient. The Court unanimously decided in 1997 that Paula Jones's civil suit against President Clinton for alleged sexual harassment could go forward, even during his White House tenure. Breyer warned in his concurring opinion that such litigation could prove highly distracting to an incumbent president. Although the trial court judge eventually dismissed the Jones case for insufficient evidence (and while it was still on appeal, Clinton settled), Special Prosecutor Kenneth Starr's collateral investigation of White House intern Monica Lewinsky's affair with President Clinton did indeed prove distracting and embarrassing for the nation's chief executive. It ultimately led to his impeachment by the House of Representatives in 1998; the Senate, however, acquitted Clinton in early 1999 after a trial presided over by Chief Justice Rehnquist. In all of the post-9/11 terrorism cases, challenging presidential power over suspects held in domestic military prisons or at Guantanamo Bay, Breyer voted in favor of requiring the chief executive to observe "democratic means,"[14] whether through judicial or legislative procedures.

Not surprisingly, given Justice Breyer's broad experience in economic regulation and administrative law, he has written a number of cases involving business practices. Indeed, his first opinion for the Court in *Allied Bruce Terminix Cos., Inc. v. Dobson* (the aforementioned termite extermination contract case) contained his broad interpretation of Section 2 of the Federal Arbitration Act under Congress's Commerce Clause power, in order to preclude a state from applying an antiarbitration policy. The Dobsons had sued the exterminating company after an inspection of their new home, covered by a Terminix contract, revealed a termite infestation. In *Qualitex Co. v. Jacobson Products, Co., Inc.*, Justice Breyer wrote for a unanimous Court that the Lanham Trademark Act of 1946 "permits the registration of a trademark that consists, purely and simply, of a color." Qualitex, manufacturers of dry-cleaning press pads with a distinctive green-gold coloring, had brought suit against their rival, Jacobson Products, for making similarly colored pads.

On jury awards in liability suits against companies, Justice Breyer wrote for an unusual line-up of Chief Justice Roberts and Justices Kennedy, Souter, and Alito. His majority opinion in *Philip Morris USA v. Williams* (2007) ruled that a jury cannot impose punitive damages against a company for harm it caused people who are not parties to the lawsuit. That same term Breyer wrote for a seven-person majority refusing to allow a private antitrust suit over Wall Street initial public offering practices during the high-tech investing bubble that burst in the early 2000s (*Credit Suisse Securities v. Billing*). He ruled against business interests in writing for the Court that federal laws protecting workers against discrimination also protect them from corporate retaliation (*CBOCS West v. Humphries* [2008]).

If one opinion could embody a justice's ideology, for Breyer it might well be his dissent in *Bush v. Gore*. He agreed with the more conservative *per curiam* opinion that Florida's chaotic recount of presidential votes in 2000 indeed violated the equal protection rights of individual voters. Yet he objected to the Court's accepting the litigation, arguing that Congress is the proper venue for settling presidential election disputes. Looking back at history, as his constitutional interpretation requires, Breyer concluded that, when the Court and Congress go head to head, the latter usually emerges victorious, to the detriment of the Court's authority and legitimacy. Finally, he believed that Florida could establish standards for the recount in a timely manner and that the U.S. Supreme Court should not have ordered the recount stopped.

Breyer's record on the high bench coheres with his previous work on the U.S. Court of Appeals and his scholarly interests in jurisprudence, economic regulation, and administrative law. Even while on the Supreme Court he has continued to teach at Harvard, contributing approximately ten sessions each year to a seminar on business regulation and administrative law at the John F. Kennedy School of Government. He has commented that he finds it "refreshing and invigorating" to meet directly with students, from whom he continues to learn in the academic fields that interest him. Moreover, Justice Breyer maintains that teaching is "a way of escaping some of the isolating features" of life in the "Marble Palace."[15]

Although critics sometimes describe Breyer as cool and aloof, he can display a genuine interest in others. And he continues to embrace life's challenges with the enthusiasm and determination that marked his youth. In his fifties, he took up Spanish, teaching himself the language through tapes that he listened to during his morning exercise routine and practicing his newfound skill with Spanish-speaking dignitaries who visit the Supreme Court. He still enjoys cycling despite his harrowing 1993 accident, when a car plowed into him as he pedaled through Harvard Yard. In 2003 Breyer, Ginsburg, and Kennedy made cameo appearances in the Washington Opera's performance of *Die Fledermaus*. Although they played judges, wearing black robes, and sitting silently on stage, Breyer commented afterward that he was "tempted to hum along" to Placido Domingo's arias![16] But Breyer truly relishes his real-life role as a judge at the pinnacle of his profession. He argues that all the work of the jurist (unlike that of the legislator) is displayed in the written fruits of his labors—the legal opinions. As Justice Breyer is fond of saying, "The inside story of the Court is that there is no inside story." Although journalists and scholars alike would disagree with that conclusion, Breyer's devotion to his craft of judging is indeed inspiring.

CHAPTER NINE

Samuel A. Alito, Jr.

The classic adage, "Third time's a charm," is especially apt for some Supreme Court justices. They were not nominated three times before successfully ascending the bench. Rather, two other unfortunate nominees ahead of them did not reach the pinnacle of the judicial hierarchy and take their seat on the tribunal. In the modern era, Justices Harry Blackmun and Anthony Kennedy succeeded where two candidates before them had failed. Blackmun finally filled a vacant seat in 1970 after President Richard Nixon's first two choices, Clement Haynsworth and Harold Carswell, went down to defeat in the Senate. Likewise, Kennedy was the last of President Ronald Reagan's trio to replace retired Justice Lewis Powell. The Senate refused to confirm Reagan's first choice, Robert Bork, and his second nominee, Douglas Ginsburg, had to withdraw when stories of his smoking marijuana while a law professor circulated in the media. Blackmun liked to joke with Kennedy that they both belonged to the "Old Number Three Club."

Samuel Alito's route to the Supreme Court was, in some ways, even more circuitous. He was on President Bush's short list to replace Justice Sandra Day O'Connor in the summer of 2005. In fact, Bush's White House Counsel Harriet Miers placed him at the top of her choices. She thought he was a safe bet to tip O'Connor's seat to the conservative bloc because of his fifteen-year record on the U.S. Third Circuit Court of Appeals. In fact, he had earned the moniker "Scalito" because of his ideological kinship with Antonin Scalia. Yet Alito is a soft-spoken, reserved intellectual who did not interview quite as well as the congenial John Roberts in his meeting with President Bush. Moreover, his much longer record on the federal bench (ten years versus two) meant that Democrats could whip up more opposition to him than for a Roberts nomination. The latter had a much shorter judicial paper trail and had been particularly adept at flying under the ideological radar. Liberals knew that Roberts was conservative, but his colleagues and friends over the years did not see him aggressively pursuing an agenda. So Roberts got the nod from Bush to replace O'Connor.

Just as Roberts's Senate confirmation hearings were about to begin, however, Chief Justice William Rehnquist died of thyroid cancer in early September 2005. Within forty-eight hours the president nominated Roberts to succeed his mentor and friend in the Court's center chair. Now Bush and his advisors were back to square one; they had to find another replacement for O'Connor. Out came the list of candidates they had considered two months previously. By most accounts, Alito had come in second to Roberts; Edith Clement and Michael Luttig had dropped out of contention after ineffective interview performances with the president; Jay Wilkinson had spoken to the *New York Times* about his interview with Bush, which probably lowered the odds of his selection. Judge Wilkinson, a brilliant protégé of the late Justice Lewis Powell, enjoyed his cordial meeting with the president, though the two had disagreed over the best exercise regimen, Bush preferring cycling and Wilkinson jogging! Miers continued to back Alito. The president had been pressed during the first search to nominate a female to the "woman's seat" on the Court; now that pressure increased, including from First Lady Laura Bush. Justice Ruth Bader Ginsburg, a pioneer in the women's rights movement, also made it known that she should not be the only female on the nation's highest court. Bush's advisors added several more names, primarily federal appeals court judges, to the original cast of characters in this nearly three-month-old Supreme Court selection drama.

Yet the president kept circling back to the woman running the search in the White House, his counsel, Harriet Miers. At first she was reluctant to contemplate her improbable selection. Yet Bush had a history of choosing long-time friends and associates for important offices. He saw her as the perfect candidate: a pioneering woman lawyer in Texas and born-again Christian, with a single-minded work ethic and conservative bent. Miers ultimately conceded to the president's wishes.

Through the timing of his announcement, Bush inexplicably overshadowed his successful appointment of Chief Justice John Roberts. Just a few hours before the new chief took the oath of office and made the traditional walk down the Court's majestic marble steps with his most senior colleague Justice John Paul Stevens, the president stunned the capital by announcing Miers's nomination to O'Connor's seat. The *Washington Post*'s lead immediately foreshadowed the problems that would follow. Although she had overcome gender barriers in the "Texas legal world," the *Post* acknowledged, "[she] brings no judicial experience or constitutional background."[1] From there, her nomination careened downhill. Conservatives turned against her from the beginning, arguing that she had no judicial track record. She might be another David Souter! Bush's father, President George H. W. Bush, had named the New Hampshire jurist to the high court, and he had assured his party's right wing that Souter was conservative. Not long after reaching the Supreme Court, however, Souter began voting with the liberal bloc. Still smarting over that error, Republicans were champing at the bit to move the O'Connor swing seat to their side of the political spectrum. Now the president had nominated an untested, unknown quantity. When Miers began her one-to-one meetings with senators, her candidacy continued its downward trajectory. She simply could not learn a career's worth of constitutional law in a few weeks. The contrast with Roberts, among the keenest legal minds of his generation, was stark.

After only a little more than three weeks, the Bush administration pulled the plug on the Miers nomination. Ironically, the president turned to the choice Miers had promoted all along, Alito. Merit and ideology ultimately trumped gender. Like the new chief justice, Alito possessed sterling credentials. Born in Trenton, New Jersey (also the birthplace of Justice Scalia), on April 1, 1950, to Italian immigrant Samuel A. Alito, Sr. and Rose Alito, he grew up in a nearby suburb, Hamilton Township. His ninety-year-old mother, a retired elementary school principal still lived in his boyhood home at the time of his appointment. Alito's late father had been a high school history teacher before becoming the first director of the New Jersey Office of Legislative Services, where he researched legislation from a nonpartisan perspective.

Samuel, Jr. and his sister Rosemary attended Hamilton East-Steinert High, where the future justice's intellect impressed his teachers. In fact, his sophomore English teacher did not think the standard curriculum posed enough of a challenge for him, so she assigned him literature by Faulkner, Orwell, Sinclair, and Kafka. She recalled after his nomination to the Supreme Court, "If I made a statement, I had better be able to defend it, because he would come back at me. But Sam was always very respectful even when he disagreed."[2] His teachers had to exclude his marks when they graded on the curve, so that he would not skew the results. Quiet, polite, scholarly—educators, mentors, and peers returned to these adjectives repeatedly to describe Alito. With a thin face, dark-rimmed glasses, and serious expression, young Alito certainly looked the part of the class brain. He served as president of the student council and editor of the high school newspaper. He excelled at debate and public speaking. Alito played in the school band and ran track. Baseball and the nearby Philadelphia Phillies sparked a lifelong devotion. Predictably, he graduated as the valedictorian of his senior class.

His next educational challenge came at Princeton, where he enrolled in the prestigious Woodrow Wilson School to study politics. Professor Walter Murphy, a renowned constitutional scholar, served as his mentor and supervised his senior thesis on the Italian Constitutional Court. He remembered that Alito "thought in judicial opinions even then."[3] As an undergraduate, Alito read approvingly Yale Law Professor Alexander Bickel's critiques of the liberal activist Supreme Court of the 1950s and '60s, led by Chief Justice Earl Warren. At Princeton young Sam joined the debate team and earned a $100 prize for presenting a defense of Vice President Spiro Agnew, who resigned from the Nixon administration after he was charged with engaging in corrupt activities while governor of Maryland. Alito's career at Princeton, from 1968 to 1972, coincided with the tumult over the Vietnam War. Rather than risk being drafted into the Army infantry after graduation, he signed up for the Reserves Officer Training Corps. His active duty consisted of only three months, but he served in the Army Reserve and received an honorable discharge at the rank of captain in 1980.

After graduating from Princeton, Alito headed to Yale Law School. One of his classmates there described him as speaking infrequently in classes, "but when he did it was something you wished you had said."[4] Another commented, "If you missed class and needed someone to borrow notes from, Sam was the person."[5] At Yale, a classmate explained after Alito's nomination to the Supreme Court, "Sam found a genuine intellectual home in the law. He likes its detail, its care, its exactitude, and he likes its fairness."[6] As a conservative, Alito was decidedly in the minority, but he sought out the few professors of his ideological ilk at the Ivy League institution, like Robert Bork, whose Supreme Court confirmation would fail in 1986. He also read the works of conservative thinkers, like William F. Buckley, and Supreme Court opinions by judicial restraintists. Despite serving as an editor of the Yale Law Journal, Alito did not receive an offer to clerk at the U.S. Supreme Court. Instead, he settled for the next best post-law school training ground. a clerkship for a federal appeals court judge. He stayed close to home in clerking for Newark-based Third Circuit Court of Appeals Judge Leonard I. Garth, a Nixon appointee and meticulous jurist.

Alito remained in appellate law at his next position as an assistant U.S. attorney in Newark, from 1977 to 1980, which allowed him to argue before the Third Circuit Court of Appeals. While a federal prosecutor, he met Martha-Ann Bomgardner, a law librarian in the U.S. attorney's office. His intellect and judicious demeanor, such a contrast to her ebullience, impressed her immediately, but it took him over a year to ask her out on a date. She thought their relationship would end when he moved to Washington, D.C. in 1981 to become an assistant solicitor general in the Reagan Justice Department. They married four years later and have two children, Phillip and Laura.

While working for the solicitor general, Alito argued a dozen cases on behalf of the U.S. government before the Supreme Court, but he avoided the ideological zealotry rampant among his colleagues. Alito was a civil service employee, while many attorneys in the s.g.'s office were political appointees. Those who served with him at the Justice Department draw distinctions between Alito and Scalia. The former was always willing to consider Congress's intent in passing a law, whereas the latter argues that a statute's wording is paramount to the vague notion of its creators' intentions. One of the colleagues from his years in the s.g.'s office describes Alito as a "conservative conservative"; he would never go to an extreme to reach his result.[7] For example, he suggested that the Reagan administration could more effectively oppose *Roe v. Wade* by supporting state restrictions on abortion as they were challenged before the U.S. Supreme Court. This evolutionary strategy would obviate the need for a more confrontational approach that called for overturning the *Roe* precedent. In addition, Alito drafted the government's brief in a case challenging race-based lay-off decisions by a Michigan school board. He compared the policy to having the fences moved closer to home plate in a ballpark, whenever Hank Aaron, the black home-run king, came to bat.

Four years after Alito's arrival in Washington, the Justice Department's Office of Legal Counsel invited him to serve there as a deputy assistant attorney general. His application to become a political appointee included his opinions on abortion rights and affirmative action. For the first time in his legal career, he committed his conservative personal perspectives to paper. Alito asserted that the U.S. Constitution does not support either a woman's right to abortion or the use of racial preferences to achieve diversity. For two years in the OLC, he provided legal advice to the Reagan administration, which was then embroiled in the Iran-contra scandal. Reagan officials had sold weapons to Iran and then used proceeds from the sale to fund anti-Communists in Nicaragua, a clear violation of the law.

Now married, and with baby Phillip in tow, Martha and Sam Alito wanted to move back to New Jersey to raise their family near their own parents. President Reagan appointed Alito to U.S. attorney for the Garden State in 1987, where litigation included organized crime, child pornography, terrorism, and corruption in the public and private sectors. Once more, he applied his meticulous, methodical, unassuming approach to highly charged issues. He diversified his staff of attorneys, not through quotas, which he opposed, but by hiring qualified minorities in the previously mostly white office. His 1990 nomination by President George H. W. Bush to the Third Circuit Court of Appeals, the bench where he had clerked fourteen years earlier, prompted accolades even from the president's opposing party. His home-state senator, fellow Princeton alumnus, Bill Bradley (D.-N.J.), and Senator Edward Kennedy (D.-Mass.) both sang his praises, and the Senate confirmed him unanimously by a voice vote.

The mild-mannered Judge Alito did not become a fire-brand once on the federal appellate bench. He continued to live up to his philosophy of not wearing his ideology on his black robe's ample sleeve. Nonetheless, during fifteen years on the Third Circuit, he produced a lengthy conservative record that ultimately earned him the trust of his appointing president's son in the Oval Office. In *Planned Parenthood v. Casey*, destined for the U.S. Supreme Court, Alito dissented from the three-judge panel's majority opinion striking down Pennsylvania's requirement that married women notify their spouses before having an abortion. The Supreme Court eventually agreed with Alito's two colleagues that such a requirement imposed an "undue burden" on women. Most important, five justices used *Casey* to reaffirm the fundamental right to abortion established in *Roe*. Alito voted to invalidate New Jersey's partial birth abortion ban, however, because the Supreme Court had already voided a similar law from Nebraska.

In religion cases, Alito, a life-long, practicing Roman Catholic, tended toward accommodation of church and state. Writing for the Third Circuit, he approved a Jersey City Hanukkah menorah and crèche display in front of city hall because the town had added a plastic Santa Claus, Frosty the Snowman, red sleigh, and symbols of Kwanzaa to demystify the religious emblems.

While on the Third Circuit, Alito fashioned opinions broadly interpreting First Amendment free speech rights. He invalidated a Pennsylvania school district's anti-harassment policy that prohibited derogatory jokes and comments about race, religion, gender, and sexual orientation. Judge Alito concluded that such bans swept too widely in preventing offensive, but protected, expression. He also defended the commercial speech of alcoholic beverage purveyors, whose ads Pennsylvania barred from university newspapers. The state had failed to prove that such a ban would diminish underage drinking on college campuses. Moreover, the newspapers themselves suffered from lost advertising revenue.

Not surprisingly, given his prosecutorial background, Judge Alito most often supported the government's position, over the defendant's, in criminal rights cases. On gun control, he authored a dissenting opinion arguing against a federal ban on assault weapons ownership. He questioned Congress's authority to pass such a law because it had not demonstrated that possession of a machine gun facilitated crimes that, in turn, had an impact on interstate commerce.

After the Miers nomination fiasco, particularly the vociferous criticism of her nonexistent experience in constitutional law and questionable conservatism, President Bush readily focused on Alito's exemplary record in announcing his nomination on October 31, 2005. Standing at a podium placed in the White House's Cross Corridor that connects the mansion's East Room and State Dining Room, the president introduced the third nominee for Justice O'Connor's seat. With Martha, Phillip, and Laura Alito looking on (ironically in front of a giant oil portrait of President Bill Clinton), Bush described the rather stunned-looking jurist to the country: "Judge Alito is one of the most accomplished and respected judges in America, and his long career in public service has given him an extraordinary breadth of experience."[8] The president cited Alito's fifteen-year tenure on the appellate bench as surpassing all Supreme Court nominees over the previous seven decades.

Stepping to the lectern with the presidential seal, Alito described his "sense of awe" the first time he argued before the nine justices on the high tribunal in 1982. "And I also remember the relief I felt when Justice O'Connor, sensing, I think, that I was a rookie made sure that the first question that I was asked was a kind one. I was grateful to her on that happy occasion, and I am particularly honored to be nominated for her seat."[9]

Senate Majority Leader Bill Frist (R.-Tenn.) pronounced Alito "outstanding," but his counterpart, Minority Leader Harry Reid (D.-Nev.), foreshadowed storm clouds, "It is sad that the president felt he had to pick a nominee likely to divide America, instead of choosing a nominee in the mold of Sandra Day O'Connor." Senator Charles Schumer (D.-N.Y.), a member of the Judiciary Committee also focused on the president's decision to bypass calls for a female justice to fill the woman's seat. "President Bush would leave the Supreme Court looking less like America and more like an old boys' club," Schumer commented.[10] Moderate Republican Arlen Specter of Pennsylvania, chair of the Senate Judiciary Committee and a supporter of abortion rights, predicted that his lead-off question to Alito at the confirmation hearings would be about his opposition to *Roe v. Wade*. Democrats immediately threatened a filibuster to block the nomination from coming to a full Senate vote.

Alito's Senate confirmation hearings were scheduled to begin just after the first of the year, so Democrats, Republicans, and interest groups had two months to mount their campaigns on the third Supreme Court nominee for O'Connor's seat. The phenomenon of "swing seat politics" now accelerated at full speed. With Roberts ensconced as chief justice, and the Court likely to split evenly among four liberals and four conservatives on controversial issues, Alito's nomination unleashed vociferous debates. The Senate arithmetic seemed clear to the White House. If Senate Republicans could unite, they would ensure fifty-five votes for the nominee. The GOP would need an additional handful of votes from moderate Democrats in the Senate to break a Democratic filibuster. To reassure senators fearing that Alito might vote to overturn *Roe v. Wade*, his former mentor and then colleague, Judge Garth of the Third Circuit, declared flatly, "[He] would not." Though Alito might restrict or limit the *Roe* precedent, "I don't think he'll overrule it," concluded Garth.[11]

As November wore on, however, the media circulated Alito's 1985 Justice Department job application, where he interpreted the Constitution as not supporting a right to abortion. In courtesy meetings with senators, the nominee attempted to distinguish between personal opinions expressed in a job search and the law-based decisions of a judge. His efforts failed to dilute liberal interest groups' opposition. Toward the end of November, they launched television ads warning, "The right wing has taken over the West Wing [of the White House]. Don't let them take over your Supreme Court."[12] Conservative groups battled back with TV and radio ads in states that voted for President Bush in 2004 but which had Democratic senators. Reminding the public that the Senate had approved Alito for the Third Circuit unanimously in 1990, the ads criticized his opponents for their "clear agenda . . . to take God out of the Pledge of Allegiance . . . [and] redefine traditional marriage. They support partial-birth abortion [and] sanction the burning of the American flag. . . ."[13]

After all the stridency and posturing surrounding the Alito nomination, the Senate Judiciary Committee hearings finally began on January 9, 2006. In his opening statement, the nominee asserted that "a judge cannot have any agenda, a judge cannot have any preferred outcome in any particular case. The judge's only obligation is to the rule of law. In every single case, the judge has to do what the law requires."[14] The heated sparring between the nominee and senators over abortion, presidential authority, judicial precedents, race, gender, federal power, states' rights, terrorism, and the death penalty spanned four days. On day three of the taut spectacle, Mrs. Alito, sitting behind her husband, left the hearing room in tears during a discussion of insinuations that Judge Alito was racist. Later reports stated that she also suffered a migraine headache. The Alitos could take heart that the first testimony presented, after questioning of the candidate ended, came from the American Bar Association's Standing Committee on Federal Judiciary, which awarded Judge Alito its highest rating, "Well Qualified."

On January 24, the Senate Judiciary Committee sent Alito's nomination to the full Senate by a split vote along partisan lines (ten Republicans to eight Democrats). Two days later, Senator John Kerry (D.-Mass) called for a filibuster of the confirmation. Senators Edward Kennedy and Hillary Clinton (D.-N.Y.), along with Minority Leader Harry Reid, supported the effort. Yet they could not muster the support necessary to keep the effort going, and the floor debate on Alito ended. On January 31, 2006, the Senate confirmed Samuel Alito by a vote of 58–42. About an hour later, Chief Justice John Roberts administered the oath of office to his newest colleague at the Supreme Court. Justice Alito donned his black robe just in time to attend that night's State of the Union Address by President Bush as a representative of the high tribunal in the Capitol's House of Representatives chamber. His face was a portrait of joy and relief.

After 24½ terms on the Supreme Court, Justice Sandra Day O'Connor officially retired. Her storied career as the first woman justice and frequent swing voter came to an end. Court observers anxiously awaited the impact of Justice Alito. In oral argument, his style contrasted with his female predecessor. From her earliest days on the bench, she had always asked several questions per case. Initially, it appeared that she had written out the questions ahead of time, so that she could display her careful preparation to the public audience. As she gained more experience, her queries became increasingly natural, flowing with the twists and turns of the oral argument. Alito remains soft-spoken, posing somewhat fewer inquiries to the counsel before the Court, but he does not hesitate to zero in on the heart of the issue. He has poked fun at his dry wit, telling the National Italian American Foundation that he should alert the press to his humor by prefacing it with "JK," the abbreviation for "just kidding," that his college-age daughter taught him in text messaging.[15]

During the partial term he served from January through June 2006, the most junior justice voted with Chief Justice Roberts most frequently (ninety percent of the time). Alito authored only nine opinions, four of which were for the majority. He voted with the Court to uphold Arizona's method of determining whether a defendant is insane, based on his capacity to distinguish right from wrong (*Clark v. Arizona*), and Kansas's statute placing the burden on capital defendants to prove that mitigating circumstances outweigh aggravating ones (*Kansas v. Marsh*). Alito was also with the majority in diluting the rule requiring police to "knock and announce" themselves before entering a dwelling to investigate (*Hudson v.*

Michigan). In the term's most sensational decision, *Hamdan v. Rumsfeld*, the newest justice sided with the three dissenters from the majority ruling that military commissions were not authorized by Congress and violated the Uniform Code of Military Justice and the Geneva Conventions. He joined the plurality who narrowed the reach of the Clean Water Act by arguing that it applied to "continuously flowing bodies of water," not wetlands (*Rapanos v. United States*).

Justice Alito's first full term on the Supreme Court (2006–07) provided a clearer picture of his position among the nine justices in the new Roberts era. As expected, he began to tip the balance to the right as he became a reliable vote for the conservative bloc, consisting of the chief justice, Scalia, Thomas, and sometimes Kennedy, who embraced the role of the tribunal's swing vote. Alito sided with Roberts ninety-two percent of the time, and seven of the fifteen total opinions he authored were for the majority. Two of these opinions for the Court attracted particular attention for their conservative outcomes. In *Hein v. Freedom from Religion Foundation, Inc.*, he ruled for the 5–4 Court that taxpayers do not have legal standing to bring law suits challenging expenditures of federal money to support the Bush administration's Office of Community and Faith-Based Initiatives. Again, for a closely divided 5–4 majority, he determined that a woman who wanted to sue her employer for gender-based pay discrimination under Title VII of the 1964 Civil Rights Act had to do so within 180 days of the alleged action. The employee, now retired, argued that the company had discriminated against her over her entire tenure (*Ledbetter v. Goodyear Tire & Rubber*). His vote was also crucial in upholding, 5–4, the federal Partial-Birth Abortion Ban Act (*Gonzales v. Carhart*). In addition, he voted with the five-justice majority to view corporate and union advertising in campaigns as core political speech, thus creating an exception to the McCain-Feingold Act's restrictions (*Federal Election Commission v. Wisconsin Right to Life, Inc.*). Alito also supported the Court's 5–4 invalidation of Seattle's and Louisville's voluntary race-based assignment of public school children to achieve racial diversity (*Parents Involved in Community Schools v. Seattle School District No. 1* and *Meredith v. Jefferson County Board of Education*). In the latter three cases, Justice O'Connor undoubtedly would have provided a fifth vote to swing the result to the opposite side.

In the 2007–08 term, Alito revealed his prosecutorial background in dissenting (along with Justice Thomas) from two seven-person majorities allowing judges more leeway in setting criminal sentences. The Court ruled that federal judges are not required by the federal guidelines to mete out longer sentences for defendants who sell crack cocaine rather than the powdered version (*Kimbrough v. United*

States) and that appellate courts should apply deferential standards to trial judges' sentencing decisions (*Gall v. United States*). In both instances, Alito supported the stiffer penalties at issue. As he had in 2006, he sided with the president in dissenting from 2008's ruling that suspected terrorists detained at the U.S. Navy base in Guantanamo Bay, Cuba, had constitutional rights to challenge their imprisonment in federal courts (*Boumediene v. Bush*). He also followed his previous opposition to gun control, while on the circuit bench, with a majority vote to strike down Washington, D.C.'s strict ban on handgun ownership as a violation of the Second Amendment (*District of Columbia v. Heller*). On the 2008 term's death penalty cases, Alito voted in the majority to uphold the three-drug protocol in lethal injections (*Baze v. Rees*) but was on the losing side in *Kennedy v. Louisiana*, which struck down the state's capital punishment law for child rapists.

Alito maintained his consistent opposition to campaign finance regulation, writing the Court's opinion in *Davis v. Federal Election Commission*, which struck down the so-called Millionaire's Amendment in the McCain-Feingold Act. By a narrow 5–4 vote, Alito voided, as a First Amendment violation, the raised caps for contributions from candidates who run against self-funded, wealthy opponents.

Although a justice's first terms on the Supreme Court do not necessarily portend his voting posture for the remainder of his career there, Alito's initial opinions and votes certainly are consistent with the conservatism he embraced as a young man and carried throughout his law career. Recently attending a gala dinner at George Washington's historic home, Mount Vernon, Justice Alito, handsomely attired in black tie and dinner jacket, quietly circulated through the crowd, while his wife chatted amiably with other attendees. When a guest remarked to the justice that it was an honor to meet him, he sheepishly replied, "Thank you." To the diner's comment that she would see him at the Court, he smiled, "That's where I'll be!" One of the most junior justice's favorite quotations from a Supreme Court opinion is Justice John Marshall Harlan II's dissent from the 1964 *Reynolds v. Sims* ruling that mandated equal numbers of voters in legislative districts. Wrote Harlan, "The Constitution is not a panacea for every blot upon the public welfare, nor should this Court, ordained as a judicial body, be thought of as a general haven for reform movements. This Court . . . does not serve its high purpose when it exceeds its authority, even to satisfy justified impatience with the political process."[16] Alito's usual deference to that process is readily apparent in most of his votes thus far. The Supreme Court's newest justice seems to have settled in comfortably to the "Old Number Three Club."

Notes

Introduction

1. These include removal of mandatory jurisdiction cases from the Court's docket by Congress in the late 1980s, uniformity of decisions in a federal judiciary guided by 20-years' worth of Reagan/Bush I and II appointees, and a more conservative Supreme Court less willing to use the law to pursue a broad social agenda. See Linda Greenhouse, "Case of the Dwindling Docket Mystifies the Supreme Court," *New York Times*, December 7, 2006, p. A1, and David Von Drehle, "Inside the Incredibly Shrinking Role of the Supreme Court: And Why John Roberts Is O.K. with That," *Time*, October 22, 2007, pp. 40–49.

2. Qtd. in York Associates Television, Inc. (producer), *The Supreme Court of the United States* (Washington: Supreme Court Historical Society, 1997), video.

Chapter One

1. Roberts's Remarks, Supreme Court Summer Institute, U.S. Supreme Court, June 24, 2006.

2. Qtd. in R. Jeffrey Smith and Jo Becker, "Record of Accomplishment–And Some Contradictions," *Washington Post*, July 20, 2005, p. A12.

3. Memo from John Roberts to Sandra Day O'Connor, National Archives and Records Administration, Record Group 60, Department of Justice, Accession #60-88-0494, Box 5, Folder: Kuhl Miscellaneous.

4. Brief for the Respondent, *Rust v. Sullivan*, 1989 U.S. Briefs 1931 (1990).

5. Bloomberg News, "Police Search Justified Roberts Says in Dissent," *Washington Post*, July 23, 2005, p. A6.

6. Qtd. in Jan Crawford Greenburg, *Supreme Conflict: The Inside Story of the Struggle for Control of the United States Supreme Court* (New York: The Penguin Press, 2007), p. 23.

7. Qtd. in Jim Vandehei and Peter Baker, "Bush Answers Gonzales Critics," *Washington Post*, July 7, 2005, p. A1.

8. Qtd. in Greenburg, p. 203.

9. Qtd. in Peter Baker, "Unraveling the Twists and Turns of the Path to Roberts," *Washington Post*, July 25, 2005, p. A3.

10. C.Q. Transcriptions LLC, "He's a Man of Extraordinary Accomplishment and Ability," *Washington Post*, July 20, 2005, p. A13.

11. C.Q. Transcriptions LLC, "Roberts's Statement," *Washington Post*, July 20, 2005, p. A12.

12. Qtd. in Dan Balz and Darryl Fears, "Some Disappointed Nominee Won't Add Diversity to Court," *Washington Post*, July 21, 2005, p. A15.

13. Qtd. in Charles Babington and Mike Allen, "Nominee Isn't Well Known to Senators Who Will Judge Him," *Washington Post*, July 20, 2005, p. A11.

14. Qtd. in Peter Baker, "President Seeks Quick Approval with Another Seat Left to Fill," *Washington Post*, p. A4.

15. Associated Press, "Roberts: 'I Have No Agenda,'" *Washington Post*, September 13, 2005, p. A7.

16. Qtd. in Linda Greenhouse, "Advice to Chief: 'To You, I'm Nino,'" *New York Times*, November 9, 2005, p. A1.

17. Qtd. in Greenhouse.

18. Qtd. in Jeffrey Rosen, "Roberts' Rules," *The Atlantic Monthly*, January/February 2007, Online, www.theatlantic.com.

19. See Roberts's majority opinion online, FindLaw, www.caselaw.lp.findlaw.com, at 21.

20. Roberts's remarks, Supreme Court Summer Institute, U.S. Supreme Court, June 25, 2007.

Chapter Two

1. Personal interview, Washington, D.C., September 12, 1985.

2. Qtd. in Stephen Isaacs, "Specialist in Antitrust Law," *Washington Post*, November 29, 1975.

3. *Miller v. School District*, 495 F.2d 658 (1974), qtd. in Robert Judd Sickels, *John Paul Stevens and the Constitution: The Search for Balance* (University Park, PA: Pennsylvania State University Press, 1988), p. 7.

4. Personal interview, Washington, D.C., September 12, 1985.

5. "Stevens Picked for Court Vacancy," (Charlottesville, Va.) *Daily Progress*, November 29, 1975, p. A1.

6. See Spencer Rich, "Ford Picks Chicago Jurist," *Washington Post*, November 29, 1975, pp. A1, A4.

7. Qtd. in Lesley Oelsner, "Justice Stevens Questions Equal Rights Amendment," *New York Times*, December 9, 1975, p. 1.

8. Qtd. in Lesley Oelsner, "Stevens Calls Court Pay Too Low; Puts His Net Worth at $171,284," *New York Times*, December 10, 1975, p. 5.

9. "An Interview with Supreme Court Justice John Paul Stevens," 39 *The Third Branch* (No. 4, April 2007): pp. 1, 10-11.

10. Qtd. in Jeffrey Rosen, "The Dissenter," *New York Times Magazine*, September 23, 2007, pp. 50-56, 72, 76-81.

11. Ibid., p. 76

12. 438 U.S. 726.

13. 521 U.S. 844.

14. Qtd. in Rosen, p. 53.

15. Qtd. in York Associates Television, Inc. (producer), *The Supreme Court of the United States* (Washington, D.C.: Supreme Court Historical Society, 1997), video.

16. "An Interview with Supreme Court Justice John Paul Stevens," p. 11.

Chapter Three

1. For a brilliant analysis of Justice Scalia's approach to interpreting the Constitution, and of the impact that his father and Roman Catholicism might have had on that approach, see George Kannar, "The Constitutional Catechism of Antonin Scalia," *Yale Law Journal* 99 (April 1990): 1297-1357. An insightful book-length study of Scalia's jurisprudence is David A. Schultz and Christopher E. Smith's *The Jurisprudential Vision of Justice Antonin Scalia* (Lanham, Md.: Rowman & Littlefield, 1996). A more recent work is James B. Staab's excellent book, *The Political Thought of Justice Antonin Scalia: A Hamiltonian on the Supreme Court* (Lanham, Md.: Rowman & Littlefield, 2006).

2. Qtd. in Ruth Marcus and Susan Schmidt, "Scalia Tenacious After Staking Out a Position," *Washington Post*, June 22, 1986, p. A16.

3. Qtd. in Irvin Molotsky, "Judge with Tenacity and Charm," *New York Times*, June 18, 1986, p. A31.

4. Kannar, p. 1314.

5. Interview with Leslie Stahl on *60 Minutes*, CBS, broadcast April 27, 2008.

6. Peter B. Edelman, "Justice Scalia's Jurisprudence and the Good Society: Shades of Felix Frankfurter and the Harvard Hit Parade of the 1950s," *Cardozo Law Review* 12 (June 1991): 1799-1815.

7. Stahl interview.

8. Qtd. in Richard Carelli, "A Speechless Scalia Puts Unlikely 'Spin' on His Conservatism," *Washington Post*, May 23, 1997, p. A27.

9. Barbara A. Perry and Henry J. Abraham, "The Reagan Supreme Court Appointees," in *Great Justices of the Supreme Court*, ed. William Pederson and Norman Provizer (New York: Peter Lang, 1992), p. 332.

10. Qtd. in Barbara A. Perry, "The Life and Death of the 'Catholic Seat' on the United States Supreme Court," *The Journal of Law and Politics* 6 (Fall 1989): 87.

11. Qtd. in "President's News Conference on Resignation of Chief Justice," *New York Times*, June 18, 1986, p. A30.

12. Ibid.

13. Qtd. in Ruth Marcus, "Rehnquist, Scalia Take Their Oaths," *Washington Post*, September 27, 1986, p. A4.

14. Qtd. in Joan Biskupic, "Scalia Sees No Justice in Trying to Judge Intent of Congress on a Law," *Washington Post*, May 11, 1993, p. A4.

15. 542 U.S. 466 (2004).

16. 553 U.S. ___.

17. Qtd. in Glen Johnson, "Deciding Abortion, Suicide Issues Is Duty of Congress, Scalia Says," *Washington Post*, March 3, 1998, p. A7.

18. 492 U.S. 490.

19. 505 U.S. 833.

20. Qtd. in Barbara A. Perry's *The Michigan Affirmative Action Cases* (Lawrence: University Press of Kansas, 2007), p. 117.

21. Qtd. in Carelli, p. A27.

22. Stahl interview.

23. Interview with Brian Lamb, on *America and the Courts*, C-SPAN, broadcast July 5, 2008.

Chapter Four

1. Qtd. in Joan Biskupic, "When Court Is Split, Kennedy Rules," *Washington Post*, June 11, 1995, p. A14.

2. Qtd. in Barbara A. Perry, "The Life and Death of the 'Catholic Seat' on the United States Supreme Court," *Journal of Law and Politics* 6 (Fall 1989): 89.

3. Qtd. in "Reagan Nominates Kennedy to Fill Court Seat," *Congressional Quarterly Weekly Report* 45 (1987): 2830.

4. Qtd. in David S. Broder, "Decider on the Court," *Washington Post*, July 6, 2008, p. B7.

5. Qtd. in Nadine Cohodas, "Kennedy Finds Bork an Easy Act to Follow," *Congressional Quarterly Weekly Report* 45 (1987): 2989.

6. "Hearing Excerpts: Kennedy on the Issues," *Congressional Quarterly Weekly Report* 45 (1987): 3130.

7. U.S. Senate Committee on the Judiciary, *Report on the Nomination of Anthony M. Kennedy to Be an Associate Justice of the United States Supreme Court*, 100th Cong., 2d sess., 1988, pp. 23, 27.

8. 491 U.S. 397.

9. 505 U.S. 577.

10. 514 U.S. 779.

11. Qtd. in Stephen G. Bragaw and Barbara A. Perry, "The 'Brooding Omnipresence' in *Bush v. Gore*: Anthony Kennedy, the Equality Principle, and Judicial Supremacy," *Stanford Law and Policy Review* 31.1 (2002): 31.

12. 539 U.S. 558.

13. Jeffrey Rosen, "The Agonizer," *New Yorker*, November 11, 1996, p. 84. Before retiring from the *New York Times* as its Pulitzer-prize winning Supreme Court correspondent for three

decades, Linda Greenhouse summarized the 2007–08 term with the headline, "On Court That Defied Labeling, Kennedy Made the Boldest Mark," June 29, 2008, www.nytimes.com.

14. An eloquent statement of Kennedy's views on these subjects can be found in the text of his speech "Law and Belief," delivered at a meeting of the American Bar Association, August 2, 1997.

Chapter Five

1. The proceedings were televised on *America and the Courts*, C-SPAN, March 30, 1996.

2. Qtd. in Tinsley E. Yarbrough's superbly researched and eloquently written biography, *David Hackett Souter: Traditional Republican on the Rehnquist Court* (New York: Oxford University Press, 2005), p. 7.

3. Warren B. Rudman, *Combat: Twelve Years in the U.S. Senate* (New York: Random House, 1996), p. 162. Rudman's book contains an entire chapter on his friendship and professional association with David Souter.

4. Qtd. in "President Bush's Announcement and Excerpts from News Conference," *Washington Post*, July 24, 1990, p. A12.

5. Qtd. in R.W. Apple, Jr., "Sununu Tells How and Why He Pushed Souter for Court," *New York Times*, July 25, 1990, p. A12.

6. Qtd. in "President Bush's Announcement," p. A12.

7. Rudman, p. 152.

8. Ibid., p. 155.

9. Qtd. in Yarbrough, p. 160.

10. Scott P. Johnson and Christopher E. Smith, "David Souter's First Term on the Supreme Court: The Impact of a New Justice," *Judicature* 75 (February/March 1992): 240.

11. David H. Souter, "In Memoriam: William J. Brennan, Jr.," 111 *Harvard Law Review* (November 1997): 1.

12. 505 U.S. 833.

13. See David J. Garrow's insightful analysis of Souter's evolving jurisprudence in "Justice Souter: A Surprising Kind of Conservative," *New York Times Magazine*, September 6, 1994, p. 36.

14. Qtd. in Henry J. Abraham and Barbara A. Perry, *Freedom and the Court: Civil Rights and Liberties in the United States*, 8th ed. (Lawrence: University Press of Kansas, 2003), p. 344.

15. Qtd. in Yarbrough, p. 231.

16. See Jeffrey Toobin's *The Nine: Inside the Secret World of the Supreme Court* (New York: Doubleday, 2007) for the Souter photo and resignation speculation.

Chapter Six

1. Clarence Thomas, "Commencement Address," *Syracuse Law Review* 42 (1991): 815. See Thomas's revealing memoir, *My Grandfather's Son* (New York: Harper, 2007).

2. "The Justice Nobody Knows," *60 Minutes*, CBS, September 30, 2007.

3. Thomas, "Commencement Address," 820.

4. Qtd. in Thomas, *My Grandfather's Son*, p. 31.

5. Thomas's remarks televised on *America and the Courts*, C-SPAN, June 17, 1995.

6. See the perceptive and sophisticated analysis of Clarence Thomas's so-called "natural rights" jurisprudence in Scott D. Gerber, "The Jurisprudence of Clarence Thomas," *Journal of Law and Politics* 8 (Fall 1991): 107–41.

7. Qtd. in Thomas, *My Grandfather's Son*, p. 213.

8. Qtd. in Barbara A. Perry and Henry J. Abraham, "A 'Representative' Supreme Court? The Thomas, Ginsburg, and Breyer Appointments," *Judicature* 81 (January/February 1998): 160.

9. Qtd. in Thomas, *My Grandfather's Son*, p. 216.

10. Ibid., p. 280.

11. Qtd. in Jeff Franks, "Justice Thomas Still Healing from 'Whipping' on Hill," *Washington Post*, February 13, 1998, p. A9.

12. Qtd. in Thomas, *My Grandfather's Son*, p. 286.

13. Qtd. in Joseph Neff, "Thomas Stands Firm in His Beliefs," *Raleigh News* and *Observer*, November 1994, p. 3A.

14. Qtd. in Dana Milbank, "Let's Do the Time Warp Again," *Washington Post*, November 16, 2007, p. A2.

15. 515 U.S. 70 (1995).

16. Perry and Abraham, p. 161.

17. Qtd. in Perry, *The Michigan Affirmative Action Cases* (Lawrence: University Press of Kansas, 2007), p. 147.

18. 539 U.S. 558.

19. Thomas delivered a bitter, blistering counter-attack against such attempts to have him toe the liberal line of many African Americans at a meeting of the National Bar Association in Memphis, Tennessee, on July 29, 1998.

20. "The Justice Nobody Knows," *60 Minutes*.

21. Qtd. in Karen Testa, "Justice Thomas Offers Advice in Visit with Schoolchildren," *Washington Post*, December 21, 1997, p. A4.

22. Thomas, *My Grandfather's Son*, p. 2.

Chapter Seven

1.   Qtd. in David Van Drehle, "Brooklyn Melting Pot Forged Future Crusader," *Washington Post*, July 18, 1993, p. A14.

2.   Qtd. in Judea and Ruth Pearl, eds., *I Am Jewish: Personal Reflections Inspired by the Last Words of Daniel Pearl* (Woodstock, VT: Jewish Lights Publishing, 2007), p. 201.

3.   Ginsburg qtd. in Robert Barnes, "Ginsburg Is Latest Justice to Reflect on Faith," *Washington Post*, January 13, 2008, p. A11.

4.   Qtd. in ibid.

5.   Ginsburg's remarks to Supreme Court Summer Institute, U.S. Supreme Court, June 18, 2007.

6.   Qtd. in Ruth Marcus, "Mystery of the Girl Sleuth," *Washington Post*, June 20, 2007, p. A19.

7.   Note from Ginsburg to Barbara Perry, April 12, 2005, in the author's possession.

8.   Ginsburg's remarks to Supreme Court Summer Institute, U.S. Supreme Court, June 16, 2008.

9.   Qtd. in Barnes.

10. Ginsburg's remarks, June 16, 2008.

11. Qtd. in Lyle Denniston, "Ruth Bader Ginsburg's Long March to VMI," speech at the Annual Spring Law Club Dinner, Baltimore, MD, May 20, 1997.

12. Elizabeth Drew, *On the Edge: The Clinton Presidency* (New York: Simon & Schuster, 1994), chapter 15.

13. Ibid.

14. Ginsburg's remarks, June 16, 2008.

15. Ibid.

16. Barbara A. Perry and Henry J. Abraham, "A 'Representative' Supreme Court? The Thomas, Ginsburg, and Breyer Appointments," *Judicature* 81 (January/February 1998): 162–63.

17. Qtd. in Neil A. Lewis, "Rejected as a Clerk, Chosen as a Justice: Ruth Bader Ginsburg," *New York Times*, June 15, 1993, p. A23.

18. Qtd. in Barnes.

19. Qtd. in Barbara A. Perry, *The University of Michigan Affirmative Action Cases* (Lawrence: University Press of Kansas, 2007), p. 146.

20. See Jeffrey Rosen's fascinating feature on Justice Ginsburg, in which he argues that she is the epitome of the pragmatic, centrist, incremental jurist, "The New Look of Liberalism on the Court," *New York Times Magazine*, October 5, 1997.

21. Ruth Bader Ginsburg, "Remarks for American Law Institute Annual Dinner, May 19, 1994," *Saint Louis University Law Journal* 38 (1994): 887.

22. Remarks televised on *Prime Time Live*, ABC, December 29, 1994.

Chapter Eight

1. See "Fleeting Fame," *Legal Times*, December 5, 1994, p. 3.

2. Qtd. in Joan Biskupic, "A Judicial Pragmatist," *Washington Post*, May 14, 1994, p. A1.

3. Qtd. in Malcolm Gladwell, "Judge Breyer's Life Fashioned Like His Courthouse," *Washington Post*, June 26, 1994, p. A18.

4. Ibid.

5. 381 U.S. 479.

6. See Lloyd Grove's "The Courtship of Joanna Breyer," *Washington Post*, July 11, 1994, p. B1, for a delightful account of the Breyers' successful partnership.

7. Qtd. in "Excerpts From Clinton's Remarks Announcing His Selection for Top Court, *New York Times*, May 14, 1994, p. A10.

8. Interview with Stephen Breyer, *Docket Sheet of the Supreme Court of the United States* 31 (Summer 1995): 3.

9. Remarks televised on *America and the Courts*, C-SPAN, June 24, 1995.

10. Stephen Breyer, *Active Liberty: Interpreting Our Democratic Constitution* (New York: Knopf, 2005), pp. 82–83.

11. *Parents Involved in Community Schools v. Seattle District No. 1*, 127 S.Ct. (2007).

12. 127 S.Ct. 2618.

13. *Printz v. U.S.*, 521 U.S. 898.

14. *Hamdan v. Rumsfeld*, 548 U.S. 557 (2006).

15. Interview with Stephen Breyer, *Docket Sheet*, 12.

16. Qtd. in Gina Holland, "Three 'Supremes' Make Cameo Appearance on Operatic Stage," *The Herald*, September 7, 2003, p. 4A.

Chapter Nine

1. Qtd. in Michael A. Fletcher, "White House Counsel Miers Chosen for Court: Longtime Aide to Bush, but Never a Judge," *Washington Post*, October 4, 2005, p. A1.

2. Qtd. in Michael Grunwald, Jo Becker, and Dale Russakoff, "Comparisons to Scalia, but Also to Roberts," *Washington Post*, November 1, 2005, p. A7.

3. Qtd. in Neil A. Lewis and Scott Shane, "Leaving the Background," *New York Times*, November 1, 2005, p. A20.

4. Ibid.

5. Qtd. in Grunwald, Becker, and Russakoff.

6. Ibid.

7. Ibid.

8. Qtd. in Elisabeth Bumiller and Carl Hulse, "Bush Picks U.S. Appeals Judge to Take O'Connor's Seat," *New York Times*, November 1, 2005, p. A1.

9. Ibid., p. A18.

10. Qtd. in "Judge Samuel Alito," About: U.S. Politics: Current Events, www.uspolitics.about. com/od/supremecourt/p/alito.htm.

11. Qtd. in Charles Lane, "Alito Respectful of Precedent, Associates Say," *Washington Post*, November 6, 2005, p. A13.

12. Qtd. in Jo Becker, "Television Ad War on Alito Begins: Liberals Try to Paint High Court Nominee as Right-Wing Tool," *Washington Post*, November 18, 2005, p. A3.

13. Qtd. in ibid.

14. Qtd. in "Bush Praises Alito in Radio Address," About U.S. Politics: U.S. Gov Info/Resources, www.usgovinfo.about.com/od/thepresidentandcabinet/a/radio011.htm.

15. Robert Barnes, "Newest Justice Tips High Court to Right," *Washington Post*, June 28, 2007, p. A15.

16. Qtd. in Dale Russakoff and Jo Becker, "A Search for Order, an Answer in the Law," *Washington Post*, January 8, 2006, p. A1.

Bibliography

General Sources on Supreme Court Justices and Cases

Abraham, Henry J. *Justices, Presidents, and Senators: A History of U.S. Supreme Court Appointments from Washington to Bush II.* 5th ed. Lanham, MD: Rowman & Littlefield, 2008.

Cornell University. Supreme Court Collection. Online. www.supct.law. cornell.edu.

C-SPAN. America and the Courts. Online. www.c-span.org.

Cushman, Clare, ed. *The Supreme Court Justices: Illustrated Biographies, 1789–95.* 2d ed. Washington, D.C.: Congressional Quarterly, 1995.

Friedman, Leon, and Fred L. Israel, ed. *The Justices of the United States Supreme Court: Their Lives and Major Opinions.* Vols. 1–5. New York: Chelsea House, 1995.

Greenburg, Jan Crawford. *Supreme Conflict: The Inside Story of the Struggle for Control of the United States Supreme Court.* New York: Penguin Press, 2007.

Northwestern University. Oyez Project. Online. www.oyez.org.

Perry, Barbara A., and Henry J. Abraham. "A 'Representative' Supreme Court? The Thomas, Ginsburg, and Breyer Appointments." *Judicature* 81 (January/February 1998): 158–65.

Street Law, Inc. Landmark Supreme Court Cases. Online. www.landmarkcases.org.

Supreme Court Historical Society. Online. www.supremecourthistory.org.

Supreme Court of the United States. Online. www.supremecourtus.gov.

Rosen, Jeffrey. *The Supreme Court: The Personalities and Rivalries That Defined America.* New York: Times Books, 2006.

Toobin, Jeffrey. *The Nine: Inside the Secret World of the Supreme Court.* New York: Doubleday, 2007.

Yalof, David A. *Pursuit of Justices: Presidential Politics and the Selection of Supreme Court Nominees.* Chicago: University of Chicago Press, 1999.

Sources on Current Justices

Samuel A. Alito, Jr.

Becker, Jo, and Dale Russakoff. "A Search for Order, an Answer in the Law." *Washington Post,* January 8, 2006, p. A1.

Bumiller, Elisabeth, and Carl Hulse. "Bush Picks U.S. Appeals Judge to Take O'Connor's Seat." *New York Times,* November 1, 2005, p. A1.

Grunwald, Michael, Jo Becker, and Dale Russakoff. "Comparisons to Scalia, but Also to Roberts." *Washington Post*, November 1, 2005, p. A7.

Stephen G. Breyer

Biskupic, Joan. "A Judicial Pragmatist." *Washington Post*, May 14, 1994, p. A1.

Breyer, Stephen. Active *Liberty: Interpreting Our Democratic Constitution*. New York: Knopf, 2005.

Farrell, John Aloysius. "Scales of Justice." *Boston Globe Magazine*, May 10, 1998, pp. 16–26+.

Gladwell, Malcolm. "Judge Breyer's Life Fashioned Like His Court- house." *Washington Post*, June 26, 1994, p. A18.

Ruth Bader Ginsburg

Bayer, L. *Ruth Bader Ginsburg*. New York: Chelsea House, 2000.

Ginsburg, Ruth Bader. "Remarks for American Law Institute Annual Dinner, May 19, 1994." *Saint Louis University Law Journal* 38 (1994): 881–88.

Lewis, Neil A. "Rejected as a Clerk, Chosen as a Justice: Ruth Bader Ginsburg." *New York Times*, June 15, 1993, p. A23.

Perry, Barbara A. "Ruth Bader Ginsburg." *Encyclopedia of World Biography*, Vol. 18. Palatine, Il.: Publishers Guild, 1995. 126–27.

Rosen, Jeffrey. "The New Look of Liberalism on the Court." *New York Times Magazine*, October 5, 1997.

Van Drehle, David. "Brooklyn Melting Pot Forged Future Crusader." *Washington Post*, July 18, 1993, p. A14.

Anthony M. Kennedy

"Anthony M. Kennedy." *1988 Current Biography Yearbook*. New York: Wilson, 1988. 289–92.

Bragaw, Stephen G., and Barbara A. Perry. "The 'Brooding Omnipresence' in Bush v. Gore: Anthony Kennedy, the Equality Principle, and Judicial Supremacy." *Stanford Law and Policy Review* 13.1 (2002): 19–32.

Cohodas, Nadine. "Kennedy Finds Bork an Easy Act to Follow." *Congressional Quarterly Weekly Report* 45 (1987): 2989.

Perry, Barbara A. "Anthony M. Kennedy." *Encyclopedia of World Biography*, Vol. 17. Palatine, Il.: Publishers Guild, 1992. 308–09.

——. "The Life and Death of the 'Catholic Seat' on the United States Supreme Court." *Journal of Law and Politics* 6 (Fall 1989): 55–92.

"Reagan Nominates Kennedy to Fill Court Seat." *Congressional Quarterly Weekly Report* 45 (1987): 2830.

Rosen, Jeffrey. "The Agonizer." *New Yorker*. November 11, 1996, pp. 82–90.

John B. Roberts, Jr.

Roberts, John G., Jr. "Oral Advocacy and the Re-emergence of a Supreme Court Bar." *Journal of Supreme Court History* 30 (2005): 68–81.

Rosen, Jeffrey. "Roberts' Rules." *The Atlantic Monthly* (January/February 2007) Online. www.theatlantic.com.

Smith, R. Jeffrey, and Jo Becker. "Record of Accomplishment–And Some Contradictions." *Washington Post*, July 20, 2005, p. A12.

Von Drehle, David. "Inside the Incredibly Shrinking Role of the Supreme Court: And Why John Roberts Is O.K. with That." *Time*. October 22, 2007, pp. 40–49.

Antonin Scalia

Brisbin, Richard A., Jr. "The Conservatism of Antonin Scalia." *Political Science Quarterly* 105 (Spring 1990): 1–29.

———. *Justice Antonin Scalia and the Conservative Revival.* Baltimore: Johns Hopkins University Press, 1997.

Edelman, Peter B. "Justice Scalia's Jurisprudence and the Good Society: Shades of Felix Frankfurter and the Harvard Hit Parade of the 1950s." *Cardozo Law Review* 12 (June 1991): 1799–1815.

Kannar, George. "The Constitutional Catechism of Antonin Scalia." *Yale Law Journal* 99 (April 1990): 1297–1357.

Kozinski, Alex. "My Pizza with Nino." *Cardozo Law Review* 12 (June 1991): 1583–91.

Marcus, Ruth, and Susan Schmidt. "Scalia Tenacious After Staking Out a Position." *Washington Post*, June 22, 1986, p. A16.

Molotsky, Irvin. "Judge with Tenacity and Charm." *New York Times*, June 18, 1986, p. A31.

Perry, Barbara A. "The Life and Death of the 'Catholic Seat' on the United States Supreme Court." *Journal of Law and Politics* 6 (Fall 1989): 55–92.

Rossum, Ralph A. *Antonin Scalia's Jurisprudence.* Lawrence: University Press of Kansas, 2006.

Scalia, Antonin, and Bryan A. Garner. *Making Your Case: The Art of Persuading Judges.* St. Paul: Thomson/West, 2008.

———. *A Matter of Interpretation: Federal Courts and the Law.* Princeton, N.J.: Princeton University Press, 1997.

Schultz, David A., and Christopher E. Smith. *The Jurisprudential Vision of Justice Antonin Scalia.* Lanham, Md.: Rowman & Littlefield, 1996.

Staab, James B. *The Political Thought of Antonin Scalia: A Hamiltonian on the Supreme Court.* Lanham, Md.: Rowman & Littlefield, 2006.

Talbot, Margaret. "Supreme Confidence: The Jurisprudence of Antonin Scalia." *The New Yorker*, March 28, 2005, pp. 41–55.

David H. Souter

Farrell, John Aloysius. "Scales of Justice." *Boston Globe Magazine*, May 10, 1998, pp. 16–26+.

Garrow, David J. "Justice Souter: A Surprising Kind of Conservative." *New York Times Magazine,* September 6, 1994, pp. 36-43+.

Johnson, Scott P., and Christopher E. Smith. "David Souter's First Term on the Supreme Court: The Impact of a New Justice." *Judicature,* 75 (February/March 1992): 238-43.

Perry, Barbara A. "David H. Souter." *Encyclopedia of World Biography.* Vol. 17. Palatine, Il.: Publishers Guild, 1992. 512-14.

Rosen, Jeffrey. "The Education of David Souter." (Louisville) *Courier-Journal,* March 21, 1993, pp. D1, D4.

Savage, David G. "Justice Souter: Quiet Scholar Is Forging New Coalition on the Court." (Louisville) *Courier-Journal,* July 10, 1994, p. D1.

Souter, David H. "In Memoriam: William J. Brennan, Jr." *Harvard Law Review* 111 (November 1997): 1.

Yarbrough, Tinsley E. *David Hackett Souter: Traditional Republican on the Rehnquist Court.* New York: Oxford University Press, 2005.

John Paul Stevens

"An Interview with Supreme Court Justice John Paul Stevens." *The Third Branch* 39 (April 2007): 1, 10-12.

Biskupic, Joan. "At Long Last, Seniority: 'Quirky' Stevens Takes Helm of Court's Liberal Wing." *Washington Post,* March 20, 1995, p. A15.

Manaster, K.A. *Illinois Justice—The Scandal of 1969 and the Rise of John Paul Stevens.* Chicago: University of Chicago Press, 2001.

O'Brien, David M. "Filling Justice William O. Douglas's Seat: President Gerald R. Ford's Appointment of Justice John Paul Stevens." *Supreme Court Historical Society Yearbook, 1989.* Washington, D.C.: Supreme Court Historical Society, 1989. 20-39.

Rich, Spencer. "Ford Picks Chicago Jurist." *Washington Post,* November 29, 1975, pp. A1, A4.

Rosen, Jeffrey. "The Dissenter." *New York Times Magazine,* November 23, 2007, pp. 50-56, 76-79.

Sickels, Robert Judd. *John Paul Stevens and the Constitution: The Search for Balance.* University Park, PA: Pennsylvania State University Press, 1988.

Stevens, John Paul. "The Supreme Court of the United States: Reflections After a Summer Recess." *South Texas Law Review* 27 (1986): 447-53.

Clarence Thomas

Collins, D.R. *Clarence Thomas: Fighter with Words.* New York: Pelican, 2003.

Foskett, Kenneth. *Judging Thomas: The Life and Times of Clarence Thomas.* New York: Morrow, 2004.

Gerber, Scott D. *First Principles: The Jurisprudence of Clarence Thomas.* New York: New York University Press, 1999.

——. "The Jurisprudence of Clarence Thomas." *Journal of Law and Politics* 8 (Fall 1991): 107-41.

McCaughey, Elizabeth P. "Clarence Thomas's Record as a Judge." *Presidential Studies Quarterly* 21 (Fall 1991): 833-35.

Perry, Barbara A. "Clarence Thomas." *Encyclopedia of World Biography*. Vol. 18. Palatine, Il.: Publishers Guild, 1995. 347–49.

"Politics, Values, and the Thomas Nomination." Symposium in *PS: Political Science and Politics* 25 (September 1992): 473-95.

Thomas, Clarence. "Commencement Address." *Syracuse Law Review* 42 (1991): 815-22.

———. *My Grandfather's Son: A Memoir*. New York: Harper, 2007.

Williams, Juan. "We Realize This Is Not About Us." An Interview with Clarence Thomas. *Time*, October 22, 2007, p. 49.

Index